On Horseshoe Street

Vijitha Yapa Publications
Unity Plaza, 2 Galle Road, Colombo 4, Sri Lanka
Tel. (94 11) 2596960 Fax (94 11) 2584801
e-mail: vijiyapa@gmail.com
www.vijithayapa.com
www.srilankanbooks.com

ISBN 955-8095-98-2

First Edition May 2005
Second Revised Edition April 2006

Printed by Tharanjee Prints, Sri Lanka

On Horseshoe Street

More Tales from the Provinces

by

Tissa Devendra

Vijitha Yapa Publications
Sri Lanka

Clattering cartload of coconut husks

ACKNOWLEDGEMENTS

My sincerest thanks to Gamini Weerakoon, Editor "The Island" and Manik de Silva, Editor "Sunday Island" who gave me every encouragement and published these articles first in their fine journals.

I must also thank Ms. Kumudini Hettiaratchi, Editor, "Sunday Times Plus" which also published some of these articles.

M.N.Samsoodeen who typed these stories has earned my thanks.

DEDICATION

with all my love
to my mother
Clarice Ruth nee Felsianes
who made a man of the boy she bore
and
to my wife
Chinta Indrani nee Mivanapalana
dearest companion of my life in the provinces
and beyond ......

NOTE TO THE READER

These memories and stories, which leapfrog through my "life and times" in Sri Lanka's outstations, are narrated in roughly chronological sequence. They begin with my schooldays in Kandy and meander through my career as a government field officer in Trincomalee, Nuwara Eliya/"Aluth Eliya" and Anuradhapura/"Puranapura". All the characters in these stories are based on real people and real happenings – but then roam out into the realms of imagination. No earth-shaking events, great achievements or notable persons strut through these pages – which are only a wryly reminiscent look at life in little towns, old Kachcheries and distant villages now transformed beyond recognition or recall.

The past is, truly, another country.

THE ARTIST

Chandramali Mahalekam was dedicated to art from her childhood as her father Kalabhushana Samaradasa Muthuhewa was a Deputy Director of Education (Art) and her mother an Art teacher. She won several awards as a student at Girls High School, Kandy and Balika Vidyalaya, Anuradhapura. After leaving school she was successful in batik and screen printing and ten of her creations embellish a cathedral in Germany. She has held two art exhibitions, one with her twin sister and one with her artist father. She devotes her spare time for painting and making greeting cards. She is married to an executive in the planting sector and is the mother of a son and daughter.

This is the first book that she has illustrated.

CONTENTS

KANDY

ON HORSESHOE STREET

We were intrigued that Kandy's oldest residents yet called it "Ladan Veediya" – Horseshoe Street – although its official name was Cross Street. Only the name was left, no memories remained of sturdy blacksmiths forging horseshoes for spirited steeds of yore. We moved into No.22 Cross Street over sixty years ago. It was quite a change for our family of four children. An upstairs house gave us plenty of room for romping around, and the new pastime of stair-jumping. It was also our first house without any garden at all. We stepped out of our verandah right on to a wide concrete pavement and found ourselves located in a long unbroken line of adjoining houses – each interestingly individual in size, style, decor and occupants. Mother was highly relieved that Cross Street was a quiet, very, bywater. Hardly any cars drove down it and our pavement was the street playground.

Our verandah had two half-walls, punctured by oval apertures, and topped by trellis screens. A wide strip between wall and trellis was good for people-watching, a fascinating introduction to the verandah way of life. Our first chore was to yell to Mother whenever a particular vendor passed this way each calling out his/her wares in a unique chant. Those were the days when the market came to the verandah.

Necessities

We rose every morning to the clattering bullock cart of the seller of coconut husks with his high decibel yodel of "Pol leli! Pol-leli! Pol-aaiiee!" Kussi-ammas (not yet an endangered species) rushed out to hail him, quarrel over quality, reject the damp and collect a basket load of dry husks for kitchen fuel.

It was a lucky day for us if the baker arrived while we children were yet at home. He carried, on his head of course, a large basket covered with shiny oil cloth and topped with a conical tin lid. He whipped off the lid to present us with a tray of mouth watering crisp and gingery bread fingers, sponge-cakes, sugar cakes and, occasionally, hot-crossbuns (for we lived in the shadow of St. Anthony's Church and many neighbors were Catholics). Once we had our ration of goodies, this tray was removed and the belly of the basket was full of soft loaves of white bread and curly crusted "seeni paan". These were for Tiffin – the daily evening spread of bread, butter, jam and cakes. Our bread was yet warm and smelt sweet as it came from the bakery round the corner in Castle Street, watched over by its owner, the capacious Mrs. Sproule.

For Mother, the most important walking "stall" was the lady who carried a wobbling tower of vegetable baskets on her head. As she gingerly lowered herself we hastened to assist her to off-load her basket-tower and spread the baskets around for selection. Refrigerators were but a distant dream and green vegetables from the villages around were bought almost daily. After the selection and ritual bargaining the "amme" tucked her earnings into her blouse and stood up with a deep sigh as we fetched her basket-tower back on to the cloth pad that cushioned her suffering head. Her straight back and tower of baskets never ceased to amaze clumsy me who could not run two yards in an egg-and-spoon race without smashing the egg!

An interesting ritual involved the buying of eggs from the wizened old "thamby", with a handkerchief deftly knotted round his head, who walked the streets with a sawdust basket full of eggs. A basin of water was brought on to the verandah and eggs were gently placed in the water. Fresh eggs were heavier and sank to the bottom. These were bought. Those that floated were judged to be "off" and rejected. There were some dubious ones that never quite sank, nor did they float on top. Old Thamby exercised all his wiles to off-load these for a lower price, but Mother firmly refused to be won over by a dubious bargain.

Wobbling tower of baskets

The milk-man delivered a standing order and called over daily on his bike with bottles chinking in khaki pouches slung from the cross bar and pillion. Mother once suspected him of "improving" the milk with water and scared the man by producing an old friend who was a Public Health Inspector. From the very next day a contrite milkman produced milk of an infinitely superior quality.

The "moru"-man was an occasional, but welcome, visitor, a dark and sturdy man whose minimal Sinhala was matched by our even more minimal Tamil supplemented by mime. His stock-in-trade was curd in cigarette tins, and sweet-sour butter-milk "moru" which he poured out into our jug from a large brass pot he carried on his head.

With the war and restrictions on imported butter, moru-man rose to the occasion and bridged the gap with a rather greasy butter he churned out and sold packed in green banana-leaves.

Luxuries

On weekends and holidays we looked out for the fruit vendors singing out their wares. While mother's interests were in such nutritious, but boring, stuff as papaws we children preferred the luscious mandarines – "narang" which came to us yet tangy from the tree and the delicious bunches of rambutan during Perahera season. We were also huge consumers of "hakuru bola" (juggery balls) a permitted indulgence as they were sold by our Ayah's father.

Barely tolerated, however, though much desired, was Bombay Mutai – that sticky sweet candy floss mysteriously spun in a glass box by yet another old Thamby.

The Chinaman was the great purveyor of real luxury. Once in a while mother used to succumb to his twangy cry of "Chaiinaa Seeelk!" and call him. He leant his bike on the verandah wall and off-loaded his large bundle, neatly wrapped in Khaki cloth. As a boy, I must confess the man's exotic appearance, and nasal accent intrigued me more than the goods he sold. But I do have hazy recollections of brilliant kimonos printed with prancing dragons and swirling chrysanthemums, beautifully hand embroidered linen and swatches of lustrous silks of incredible softness. Intricate little knick knacks of ivory – fans, combs and serviette rings were also temptingly on display. Once selections were made the silks were measured out, under mother's watchful eye, with the cubit long baton the Chinaman carried both for measurement and self-defence. This baton was useful to threaten the scallywags who often ran behind him yelling "Cheenaa Booku, Booku" – which war-cry was reputed to enrage all Chinamen.

My favourite verandah salesman was the bookseller, neatly dressed in verti, who travelled around on his bike with used books piled on his pillion. He had an uncanny knowledge of a reader's tastes and budget and was perceptive in the books he offered you – and also generous to a book-hungry browser like me.

Surprisingly, father too discovered a little tapped stratum of traditional crafts when an itinerant vendor unwrapped before him beautiful lacquer "bulath-heppuwas" and necklaces of ancient design in blackened silver and agate. Our man who came from a village of traditional craftsmen, was a good raconteur. To our amazement this shabbily dressed man had travelled all over Germany and France.

German circus

The famous German circus impresario Hagenbeck had hired a band of Kandyan craftsmen, dancers and jugglers with whom he toured Europe, as sideshows to his menagerie of exotic beasts. Old Elaris was introduced by father to all his friends up from Colombo. The traditional craftsmen he promoted have long since faded away, but their richly coloured and beautifully crafted lacquer objects yet gleam quietly in the family homes of father's many friends.

Alms and processions

Beggars were among our verandah visitors – but only on Thursdays. This was on account of the Meera Makkan Mosque which dominated the skyline not far away – and had set apart Thursday for alms-giving. On their way back from Muslim generosity the beggars also visited other homes on Horseshoe Street. We children sat on the verandah presiding over a large basket of coarse rice. Every beggar came equipped with a long sling-bag into which we doled out rice with an empty cigarette tin (It is only now that I realise how ubiquitous these little objects were in daily life of yore – as a scoop, a measure of grain and oil, a container of curd, and in infinite guises in children's games.)

Occasionally we had a colourful bearded gent in orange dhoti, festooned with seed rosaries, with a brass pot on his head. He always performed a dainty pirouette tinkling a little brass bell. This pilgrim, walking to Kataragama, was the only mendicant honoured with a coin. The rest got rice. And if our basket ran out, in that gentler age, we never brusquely said "Nothing" instead "Samaa Venna" – Pardon us please.

Processions wound their colourful way down Horseshoe Street. Corpus Christi always fascinated us Buddhists with the spectacle of richly dressed "English-speaking" Catholics kneeling humbly in the asphalt street to pray. A wonderful Muslim procession originated from Meera Makkan Mosque. We called it the "Koodu Perahera" where enormous pagodas of paper and cloth were carried on the shoulders of the faithful and followed by dervishes whirling in a trance to the throb of a hypnotic drum and religious chants. The glory of the Perahera needs no description. But we on Horseshoe Street shared a brief moment of ownership when the elephants, dancers and chieftains passed but a few feet away from our very own verandah casting a transient spell of enchantment over us goggle-eyed children.

... Memories of a way of life long gone the way of the phantom horses whose hooves were once shod on Horseshoe Street.

"ROCKFIST ROGAN, PLEASE STEP FORWARD!"

War entered our lives in 1939 as ten year olds in Mrs. Coswatte's class in Dharmaraja. For schoolboys in Kandy it was great fun. A brave new world dawned new games (commandos, bayonet charges, mock air raids), new souvenirs (NAAFI cigarettes, tin hats, web belts, shoulder flashes), new foods (corned beef, tinned butter), new words and phrases (fag, dog-fights, Jerries, V for Victory and, of course, the F word).

Before the War the military world intruded on our lives only fleetingly, once a year, on Armistice Day when a cannon boomed out at 11 a.m. and the town ground to a halt for two minutes, obeying the signal of burly traffic sergeants. Poppy wreathed planters' cars halted to disembark their prim English passengers who doffed their topees and bowed their heads in reverence, rickshawmen downed shafts, irreverent cart bulls spattered the road in relief, cyclists and pedestrians uneasily shuffled their feet – bemused participants in this Colonial ritual.

In school we sprang to our feet at the cannon's first roar. Any distraction was preferable to Charavanamuttu's "Speed Tests in Arithmetic." Loyal scions of a proudly Buddhist school dominated by portraits of the patriot Sir Baron Jayatilleke resplendent in barrister's robes, and the handle-bar moustache Billimoria, Parsi pillar of Buddhist education, - we were unbelieving participants in this Remembrance Day ritual.

We kept glancing surreptitiously at the large Seth Thomas clock (why Seth and not Saint, I used to wonder) waiting for the cannon's next boom and the instantaneous bustle from the briefly silent streets. But our silence for two whole minutes was firmly guaranteed by the persistent rumour that plain clothes policemen lurked with hidden batons to crack the skulls of the disloyal who violated the sacred silence. Every boy had an uncle who had witnessed such an episode. At the cannon's second roar we slipped back into our seats, grateful for the opportunity of a stolen glance at the all correct solutions of the more numerate among us.

Afternoon saw us at the Police Parade Grounds. Soldiers in buttoned up tunics, wound-up puttees and domed pith helmets (yet sported by today's police motor cycle escort) clomped behind the oompahs of the Police Band in pill box hats and smartly saluted the remote, lanky figure of the British Government Agent resplendent in his brass buttoned white uniform and ostrich plumed helmet. That was the sum total of our pre-war military experience.

Subversive Influence

Not long after war broke out far, far away in distant Europe, a subversive influence insinuated itself into our schoolboy lives, and changed our world view for ever. This was 'Champion' the unforgettable magazine for boys. It was an English weekly printed on murky newsprint in war utility miniscule type and sporting a glossy cover in red, blue and yellow typically showing a German fighter plane being shot down in flames by a cheerful RAF pilot in a Spitfire (what else?). No gore, no disembowelling – all good, clean, British fun. Another cover would show a whole battalion of sheepish Nazis in bucket helmets led by their monocled, duel-scarred and jack-booted officer being rounded up by one or, at most, two muscular British servicemen brandishing (naturally) tommy guns and guffawing triumphantly. Yusuf's Corner Book Stall in King Street was the source of all our 'supplementary reading' (today's ghastly buzz-word), for which we illicitly, and enthusiastically, bartered our dog-eared text books. It was a poky little corner shop of creaky overloaded bookshelves and open boxes stuffed with a maddening cornucopia of old books. Old Yusuf presided over this treasure trove, a benign, grizzled figure with a sharp eye for reader preferences, adept at creating tastes and pushing his wares to book-hungry schoolboys.

Before the war he had whetted our appetites first with 'Beano', starring Desperate Dan, Keyhole Kate, Lord Snooty and their ilk. We soon left behind their childish high jinks for 'Film Fun' illustrating the mishaps of comedians of times long past – the great stand-up (and fall-flat) comics Stan Laurel and Oliver Hardy and even shadowier figures such as Joe E. Brown and Lupino Lane. But the distant rumble of war drums in Europe led us bewitched to the glorious adventures and mayhem chronicled in the unforgettable pages of Champion.

Cadetting

Meanwhile cadetting, in which Dharmaraja excelled, acquired an added glamour. Under the snappy orders of our hero Mr. (later Colonel) H.A.Perusinghe we drilled with enthusiasm. We formed fours (an archaic maneuver), marched, and smartly wheeled within the hallowed precincts of the Natha Devale, which adjoined our school, and the bridle paths of the Uduwattakelle Sanctuary with which we Rajans had a symbiotic relationship. It gave us clusters of 'kukul kakul', a droopy red flower which was a deliciously acid snack. And 'toku gedi', long-stemmed, hard and knobbly fruits which were traditional weapons in duels fought according to time-honoured rules. The loser was chased round the school and smartly rapped on his skull by the victor's weapon.

Cadetting beckoned us towards the war and excitement glamourised in Champion's print-crammed pages. We drilled with gusto looking forward to our formal parades in leather belted shorts, cocked felt hats, vivid black and yellow shoulder straps and knee stockings, steel tipped boots (from Banda's Boot Works) – which finery proclaimed our regiment, the Junior C.C.B. (Ceylon Cadet Battalion). Our new games were war games. English vs. Germans replaced 'hora-police'. Slit trenches, dug for protection against air raids, became our Maginot and

Siegfried Lines. Listing the makes of exotically camouflaged trucks and personnel carriers became a hobby as they passed in endless convoys to camps up north. Identifying the assorted races of allied soldiers became a challenge – Britishers, Aussies, African Askaris (reputed to the cannibals, and best avoided), Sikhs, Dogras, Gurkhas and (much later) Yanks.

Thanks to old Yusuf and his never ending supply of battered Champions (how they reached him across the U boat infested seas remains one of life's unsolved mysteries) we already had an interestingly skewed vision of the war by the time Mountbatten's cohorts ensconced themselves in the Botanic Gardens of Peradeniya. No wonder that Mervyn de Silva, one of our number, became the country's best known foreign affairs expert!

True Grit

Rockfist Rogan RAF exemplified all the values that Champion stood for – true British grit apotheosised as hand to hand combat. Young Rogan was a burly Squadron Leader and a formidable boxer whose pugilistic prowess earned him the name Rockfist. Through his adventures we had shadowy glimpses of life in the British forces – bullying drill sergeants, horseplay in the barracks, snooty upper crust officers, scrambling for planes, dog-fights in the clouds. The very names of planes were redolent of romance – the pugnaciously British Spitfires, Mosquitoes and Wellingtons versus the sinister sounding, German Messerschmits, Stukas and Junkers (Champion blanked out all references to Fokkers!). Rockfist's mascots were his boxing gloves and he always flew with them in his cockpit – ready to don them and fight his way out if, and when, he crash landed behind enemy lines. Many were his adventures which always culminated in a stand-up and slug-it-out-boxing match where he regularly K.Oed the bigger and burlier villain – invariably rejoicing in delightfully alliterative names as Battleship Braddock, Hulking Herman or Iceberg Ivan – evocative of brute force.

Age dims the memories of specific escapades but a few stand out. Rockfist was once shot down behind German lines and held as a P.O.W. in the usual sinister Stalag Luft. He rapidly organised the spunky British P.O.Ws and manoeuvered a boxing bout with the hulking, brutal Gestapo camp commandant whom he floored with his standard K.O. and escaped with all his buddies – light years before Steve McQueen's "Great Escape." On another occasion he flew to Finland to aid the brave Finns against the invading Russkies. Single-handedly he dropped canisters of vitriol on frozen Lake Ladoga across which the Red hordes were advancing. He drowned the rotters. Not very much later, I seem to recollect Rockfist flying sorties to rescue his beleaguered Russian allies in Stalingrad (those who had survived the Ladoga debacle). Rockfist's hapless victims, the Germans of Champion's simple universe, were glorious villains of the deepest dye. Their conduct, uniforms, phraseology and undiluted skullduggery remain so embedded in my subconscious that I can never, yet, resist any thriller on the last days of the Third Reich. They were readily distinguishable in Champion's disarmingly naive illustrations. Apart from their tightly buttoned grey uniforms and bucket helmets their expressions were invariably brutal (soldiers), supercilious (officers), leering (Gestapo) or hangdog in surrender (all ranks) after being at the wrong end of Rockfist's mighty fists. Their language was our first foray into multilingualism and greatly enriched our vocabulary of insults. Who could cap the Hunnish ferocity of 'Dumkopf', 'Schweinhund' or 'Donner and Blitzen'? But they all ended with their hands in the air as they shrieked 'Kamerad!' in abject surrender.

Rockfist, or some of his fellow heroes in Champion, flew some sorties in North Africa where they rapidly made mincemeat of the spaghetti-eating Italians. These poor chaps ranked in Champion's hierarchy, far lower than its Nazis. They were always shown in shabby uniforms, bleary-eyed and unshaven and much given to surrendering in droves, incompetently led by rotund officers in fancy uniforms. Champion's was a disarmingly puritan world. No girls ever sullied its pages or distracted its heroes from their dedicated mayhem. Nor did these swashbuckling heroes ever step into a bar-room. It was a world of comrades-in-arms whose only emotions were loyalty and patriotism.

Champion had features other than Rockfist Rogan but they have slipped away unremembered through the sieve of memory. Many were similar yarns of defeating German soldiers or outwitting Nazi spies. These were leavened with yarns where incredibly upper class public school boys made mayhem against ritual (but harmless) villains as Headmasters, Science Masters (old Stinky), French Masters, school porters, fat boys and town ruffians. But this was wishy-washy pap compared with Rockfist's slugging matches and dog-fights.

A rival publication, Triumph, briefly appeared to joust with Champion – but it soon 'hit the canvas' as all Rockfist's rivals did. It's hero was Mad Carew, a more conventional hero – conventional good looks, RAF moustache, flyer's silk scarf et al. His sole claim to remembrance is that, in his honour, we briefly renamed our classmate 'Rowdy' (a tremendous insult, that) Karu as 'Mad' Karu. But neither the new nickname nor the magazine lasted long.

Finis

The years drew on, we grew older, the war dragged on to its end, and the sun set at last on the British Empire. Rockfist was tucked away into the deep recesses of fond memory. He flickered momentarily in a Champion Annual manning an RAF outpost in a faraway southsea island of the diminished Empire. There, I seem to recall, he clobbered the native Kanaks into slugging each other according to Queensberry rules instead of eating each other for dinner!

Almost half a century has passed, Spitfires are museum pieces occasionally trundled out for nostalgic fly-pasts. But the war drums beat again and hot blood must be coursing through the veins of Rockfist Rogan's yet magnificent hulk as he hears the roar of Tornadoes revving up to smash yet another unshaven upstart of a lesser breed. It's time to stop this rot. Will Rockfist Rogan RAF please step forward to clobber Slugger Saddam and save the world? Seconds (Yanks, Frogs and assorted Wogs) out of the ring. Rockfist will prevail and all will be well.

(1994)

P.S.
Alas! this war, Desert Storm, ended before this call to arms (fists?) could be published.

YELLOW BOARDS AND WOODEN CLOGS

DHARMARAJA 1936 – 1943

If I ever sport an old school tie I will be proclaiming disloyalty to the six other schools where I studied. I must confess, however, that I left my heart behind at Dharmaraja. Family lore has it that I left behind my brains as well ..... in the stone drain into which I plunged, head first, from an overgrown tennis court by the Principal's Bungalow which we shared with the Kularatnes. Gopal, the groundsman, carried my limp body home to a hysterical mother and a long convalescence. Among my visitors was Miss Robinson, a stately Englishwoman in a flowing white dress, who lived the life of a Buddhist hermit in a little stone cottage donated by the school. She read me Jataka tales and plied me with vegetable soup. Her neighbour on the Hill was the yellow-robed Sister Dhammadinna, an amiably eccentric American millionairess, who shared her cottage with a pack of stray dogs rescued from the dog-catcher.

Way back in 1936 the college was yet in Palace Square. Only the Principal and the Boarders lived on the Hill. Outside the magnificent Vahalkada, the college shared with the Natha Devale, clustered peddlers selling velvet 'gal syambala', colourful penholders with fancy nibs and vivid water pictures we laboriously spit-pasted in our tattered textbooks. Banda's assembly bell shooed them off and summoned us to Billimoria Hall. Class by class we lined up for assembly. Kindergarten babies up front and the hulking (so they seemed to us) Prefects of the London Matric in the last row. The junior class lined up in front of us had the misfortune to contain a couple of girls. Every morning a shoving match erupted in our row as no boy ever wanted to be caught

Magnificent Vahalkada and College Hall

in the humiliating spot right behind a girl. Ours was invariably a ragged broken line – the gaps marking girl-blighted spots. While Principal Metthananda, remote and regal in his formal cloak, led us in observing 'pansil', Headmaster Mediwake prowled the classrooms for lurking latecomers whom he lined up and briskly caned.

The pompous portraits of primly dressed Principals which looked down upon us were enlivened by an intriguing picture of a bare-chested chieftain. This was the courageous Wadugodapitiya who had boldly felled an old bo tree which had obstructed the expansion of the school, proclaiming that a school served Buddhists better than any tree.

Rituals and Readers

Rituals of Edwardian correctness were dinned into us until they became reflexes. Whenever in town we Rajans kept our eyes peeled for teachers to nip down by-lanes and escape the compulsory greeting of "Good morning/evening, Sir/Madam". Slow-footed and short-sighted, the fast dodge was beyond me. I had yet another handicap – the hat I was compelled to wear after my fall. It was bad enough wearing the class football; what was worse was having to doff it to every teacher I met, every bhikkhu and also the Dalada Maligawa whenever I passed it on my way to school!

Dharmaraja was open-hearted and tolerant. Its staff and students were drawn from all races and religions. But as a Buddhist school our unstated aim was to outdo the missionary schools in everything they did – in examinations, at athletics, at cadetting and at all the team games that colonial schoolboys played. My hazy recollections are that we were top dogs in Kandy, in every field, during this era. Vague memories are far sweeter than hard facts!

The Colonial Department of Education drew up the syllabuses we followed. Most of our Readers came from England and pictured idyllic scenes of rosy-cheeked farmers, frolicking lambs, cheery Bobbies, gabled cottages and, our top favourite, Robin Hood. I recollect our sneers at the Indian based Himalaya Readers featuring dhoti-clad postmen, bullock carts and turbaned Maharajas when they replaced our vision of a pastoral Britain. The most borrowed library books were Tom Brown's Schooldays type of yarns and G.A.Henty's rousing tales of British campaigns against lesser breeds (coloured, of course). Colonial education had made a fine art of instilling sahib reflexes in little brown boys – even those in Buddhist schools.

My father, who taught history, strove to restore some sense of balance by leading school excursions to our ancient historic sites. The robust camaraderie of those cramped bus-rides, roughing it out at the homes of hospitable old boys, the stiff climbs and the vivid realness of ancient history interpreted by an enthusiast – were a feature as regular in the Dharmaraja calendar as our matches with Kingswood, cricket (which we won) and football (which we lost). What remains is an abiding awareness of our heritage, a drowsy memory of sing-songs in swaying buses and the remembered tang of corned beef and bombay onion sambol.

Dharmaraja was strong in cadetting. To the stentorian 'Eipe! Eite!' of our cadet masters our scruffy platoons were relentlessly wheeled and marched within the hallowed precincts of the Natha Devale, below the King's Palace where the G.A. lived, and beneath the green arches of the Udawatte Kele. Our days of glory were our parades in the resplendent uniform of the C.C.B. (Ceylon Cadet Battalion). The Juniors wore shoulder flashes and knee stockings of black and yellow, topped off with a cocked hat. The seniors wore Boer War uniforms with high domed topees and puttees. We all marched along to the clickety-click of steel-tipped boots, a speciality of Banda's Boot Works.

Long-suffering lady teachers dinned into our grasshopper minds nuggets of exotic information such as how beavers built their dams, when King Alfred burnt the cakes and why Archimedes leapt out of his bath-tub. Gentle romances blossomed among young teachers, gleefully spied on by us. Our religious education was the responsibility of the genial Asgiriya Hamuduruwo who almost always asked us to choose between a *'bana kathawa'* or a *'gama kathawa'*. Little '*bana*' did we know at the end of it!

We welcomed Banda's intrusions into classes carrying a stone jar of ink to fill the ink-wells on our battered desks. He also took around notices to be read out announcing college matches, annual inspections by a team of School Inspectors (dreaded by the younger staff), and the feared date for the mass administration of the ghastly purgative – *'Chinna Podiyan'.* One of our number was regularly escorted by Banda to the Headmaster for the mandatory caning for 'cutting school'. His speciality was to disappear during the tea interval, flog a textbook for a pittance with which he hired a bike for joyriding till detected by a teacher. A free soul, he assured us that the thrill of the ride far outweighed the pain of the cane. The other punishable offence was to be observed in a cinema gallery unescorted by a parent.

Up the Hill

Metthananda had the foresight to see the school outgrowing the site in town and built a handsome new building on the Hill that Billimoria had acquired from a run-down estate. The seniors moved in soon after WWII broke out. The boarders, who had always lived on the Hill, flaunted a sense of ownership over the new building much resented by the town boys who now had to trudge wearily up the hill to classes. The glorious view and airy classrooms of the new building were a welcome change. However, the most revolutionary change was the absence of blackboards and white chalk whose squeak and dust had been an integral part of our school lives. The boards in our new classrooms were a brilliant YELLOW and the chalk was bright BLUE!! and came in boxes labelled 'Cornflower Blue Chalk for Primrose Boards'. Our Principal had absorbed the latest educational theory – that it was bad for students' eyes to look up from black print on a white page to confront white script on a black board. In this era of Magiboards it is clear that Metthananda was fifty years ahead of the times. The yellow boards were great fun while they lasted but, alas, not for long. German U Boats curtailed shipping and cornflower blue chalk did not qualify as an essential commodity. The yellow boards – our badge of distinction – became another casualty of wartime. They were blacked out like the lights of Kandy at night – and the dust of white chalk came back to haunt our nostrils.

The rains which lashed our open corridors inspired a rough new game. Early arrivals lined the corridor, face to face, compelling latecomers to run the gauntlet, shoved mercilessly from side to side and skating helplessly on the rain slippery floor till they reached the end of the line to become enthusiastic pushers themselves. Great fun, but too rambunctious to be tolerated, and its ban was inevitable.

Cheekily familiar with the new building, the boarders took liberties with impunity. When dhobies went missing ("dhoby-strike" was the phrase) senior boarders weathered the crisis in College blazers with mufflers tucked in to conceal shirtlessness. This was tolerated, though grudgingly. Clogs were another story. Decades before the emergence of rubber flip-flops, heavy wooden clogs were standard household wear. Our boarders set the trend of wearing them to school. The fad spread like wildfire and the boarders' massed entry into the corridors thundered like the Charge of the Light Brigade, drowning all other sounds. Before long the Principal announced at assembly a ban on all clogs.

Evacuees and Food Production

The War brought Dharmaraja some migratory bodies – one genuine refugee and many "evacuees". Hans was a German Jewish boy whose blonde hair and woollen clothes made him gaped at during his brief stay with us. The Japanese air raid on Colombo brought us home-grown "evacuees" fleeing the feared invasion. These (to us) foppishly dressed chaps who clustered together and spoke English to each other (we didn't) were greeted with the cold shoulder and exaggerated crudity. But boys are infinitely adaptable. As time wore on these once exotic species took on the protective plumage of their rougher new environment and were welcomed in out of the cold.

The War provided the opportunity for the multifarious talents of Mr. Dharmakeerthi, our Handicrafts Master, to blossom. He was determined to use us to develop substitutes for imported objects no longer available. We had a glorious time mucking around and producing unrecognizable monstrosities of no earthly use. The outstanding feature of our products was that they stank, most foully, on account of the glue (of our own make) that held them together. We made crowns, sceptres and thrones for school theatricals. Actors could hardly be heard as the poor chaps were too busy holding their breaths fighting the all-pervasive stench. Our one real triumph was the cover of handmade paper for the 1941 College Magazine. It lies on my desk as I write, shabbily proud to have held together for 52 years.

Dharmaraja's cursory nod towards the wartime Food Production drive was to allot each class a plot of land to grow crops (I know not what). Clearing the shrub, we joyously unearthed coconut seedlings on which we furtively feasted for many weeks. The sloping hillside and heavy shrub was ideal for waging ritualised class wars of clods and stones. In one such skirmish I left behind half a tooth on the battlefield .... to further cement my links with Dharmaraja.

But nothing is for ever. Our family left Kandy and I bade a reluctant farewell to my friends in Dharmaraja, my spectacles misted with unshed tears.

Over half a century later, through the rosy mists of nostalgia, I glimpse a vision of my boyhood friends romping, once again, the classrooms and playing fields of Dharmaraja. A vision of glorious boyhood, fixed for ever in the uncorrupting amber of fickle memory.

WHO REMEMBERS ARTHUR MEE?

The name "Arthur Mee" today vaguely suggests a legislator from Hong Kong. But, many decades ago, it was a name to conjure with in the dusty magic of school library shelves. Every one of the six schools, I passed in and out of, had one whole section reserved exclusively for an impressive array of volumes, bound in blue and gold, emblazoned (with charming immodesty) Book of Knowledge Volume I to XII (or was it XXIV? – memory falters). Their editor was Arthur Mee, so un-English and exotic a name that it remains indelibly etched in memory.

Succumbing to the blandishments of slick marketeers, today's board-rooms and mansions display bookshelves crammed with yards of encyclopaedias, untouched and unread. I salute in gratitude their forbears, those booksellers of yesteryear (Apothecaries? Bastians? Makeens? Wahids?) who persuaded cash-strapped school principals to stock their libraries with Arthur Mee's Books of Knowledge. Legions of schoolboys (no info re the other gender) had their eyes opened to a far wider world, than their textbooks dully described, by the rich variety of stuff in these well thumbed volumes.

I confess that I write entirely from memory (probably flawed, definitely rosy) as I have not seen a single of these volumes for over fifty years. They were a rich treat, in those days when print was our only window to the world. Their coverage was universal and encyclopaedic but eminently readable. Their format sandwiched abridged versions of classics, memorable poems, folk tales of many lands, with informative accounts of great writers, heroes, artists, explorers and scientists. Notable inventions and scientific discoveries were interspersed with glossy plates illustrating the wonders of ancient civilizations (of these, more anon).

The "great writers" selected were, inevitably, governed by the taste of that era and judged to be enlightening, inspiring, and (of course) safe for those readers of formative years. The only names that swim into my consciousness are R.L.Stevenson and Sir Walter Scott. Shakespeare was, naturally, there.

As for poetry I seem to remember some of Tennyson's more tuneful stuff, Christina Rossetti's romances and Walter de la Mare – remembered because I was long puzzled as to why he was named after a she-horse! Poor old Scott of the Antarctic starred as the epitome of British grit.

I recall the sad image of Hudson cast adrift in the Arctic by his mutinous crew. Yet another painting that persists in memory was titled "When did you last see your father?" and depicted the plucky little son of a Cavalier stubbornly silent before his Roundhead inquisitor.

Mee, I am sure, was firmly anti-Roundhead as were most novelists we read e.g. Baroness Orczy. Tutankaman's golden sarcophagus and the excavation of his wondrous treasures by Howard Carter were imprinted on our malleable young minds.

Not long ago, rambling the woods around a friend's cottage in up state New York we came across a beaver dam. Dormant information surfaced in a flash, and I surprised my friend with my seeming expertise on life among the beavers. But I gave full credit where it was justly due – Arthur Mee, of course.

In these volumes all subjects were thriftily covered in one or two pages – or so I recall. Old Arthur was sensibly aware of the fickle span of a schoolboy's attention. All articles were copiously illustrated by very detailed drawings. The more modern (i.e around 1930) items carried rather fuzzy photographs – harking forward to those that once sprinkled the dreary publications of the defunct Soviet Union. A medley of pictures floats in my mind's eye – frock coated gentlemen in pince-nez spectacles, bearded (if French or German) standing solemnly before strange machines or quaint laboratory equipment of mysterious purpose (now found only in the labs of mad scientists in the world of comics).

From these volumes my generation picked up much of the trivia that we insinuate, with varying degrees of success, as derived from deep and serious study. It was, inevitably, a very Anglo-centric perspective that we absorbed – of the British Queen Boadicea who defied Caesar, the relief of Lucknow from blood thirsty Indian mutineers, the defeat of Chaka the Zulu and his hordes, Robert Bruce and the spider, King Alfred and the cakes, and so on ad infinitum. Good roistering stuff for schoolboy readers.

We in colonial Ceylon were just a little speck in the huge swathes of red that coloured the world maps that hung on our classroom walls. Most of my schools were Buddhist, in the heyday of revivalism, and we marched to a different drumbeat from our peers in missionary schools proudly loyal to the Brits. However, in spite of "Pansil" at assembly and "ata sil" on Poya days all our text books were from England and, inevitably, coloured our "world view".

Adolescence gradually crept up on us. Burgeoning hormones fuelled an intense curiosity with the female form. Once again it was to the Books of Knowledge we turned with avid eyes in search of enlightenment. Their pages were never sullied with explanations of the "facts of life". But their glossy plates abounded with that staple of Greek and Roman sculpture and robust Renaissance paintings – the unclothed female.

Curious adolescents gawped wide-eyed at cold marble Venuses and Rubens' romping nudes, alert to flip the page to a more acceptable educational subject whenever the library master soft-footed his way among the teenagers with studious heads buried deep in Books of Knowledge pondering the improbability of such luscious forms ever filling the starched white school uniforms we saw daily tripping along to girls' schools.

Who remembers Arthur Mee?

I do.

HEAVY POUNDERS, BITTER MEDICINES, BATTERED BUTTONS

The other day my little grand-daughter dragged me along with her to her mother's kitchen to inveigle a forbidden fistful of maldive fish chips. As I stood marooned in the surgical sterility of a modern kitchen with its ceramic tiled floors, fitted cupboards, gleaming sinks, hissing cooker, whirring mixers and humming refrigerator it struck me that, apart from the genetic predilection for maldive fish, everything around me was as absolutely different from the kitchen of my childhood as the space shuttle is from the long-forgotten rickshaw.

The kitchen of that pre WWII era was, even in urban "middle class" homes, a dark and smoky place located rather away from the living area. It was the domain of the "kussi-amma" who was never called by her given name. In the prevalent English idiom she was referred to as "the cookie" with the cheery insensitivity of class that renamed all ayahs "Jane" and houseboys "Banda". I must confess that my memories are as smoky as the kitchen of old as no man or boy ever, or rarely, crossed its threshold.

The steady pounding beat of pestle and mortar (the kitchen variety!) was the background music of our childhood. The smooth rhythm of the "mole-gaha's" rise and fall was fascinating to watch as Kussiamma pounded rice grains into flour for hoppers, roti and pittu. There was also a little mortar (vangediya) for pulverising chillies and other spices. I was a ready volunteer when it came to pounding chunks of maldive fish into chips, the fall-out carefully gathered on the newspaper on which the mortar stood. More than the "pounder's portion" went into my watering mouth. We also had a kurakkan-

Pounding beat of pestle and mortar

gala, a fascinating handmill of granite which ground the kurakkan and other cereals from the Vanni chenas which found their way to our kitchen to enliven our palates.

The kitchen proper was dark and smoky. An opening in the roof, sheltered by its own little roof, served as a not-very-effective chimney. Below it was the masonry kitchen platform on which stood three or four brick fireplaces. Above it swung a hammock of rope holding such light kindling as dried coconut spathes. The hollows beneath the cooking platform were the fuel store, stocked with firewood and coconut husks. These were the home and playground of rats who were the target groups for large rat-traps of wire mesh baited with slivers of coconut. Every morning Municipal labourers collected these traps which held the rodent prisoners and carted them off to their doom.

All cook pots ("haeli-valan" – in Sinhala, "chattypots" – in English) were clay, blackened with use. Curries simmering in them were stirred with heat-proof spoons of coconut shell – which hung on a reed woven spoon holder hanging on the smoke dimmed walls. Every kitchen was equipped with a two-foot length of iron piping which was blown to fire up dying embers. We children competed for the privilege of blowing this pipe – and ended up with ash in our eyes.

The "pittu bamboo" of old was just that, not a metal contraption. A length of seasoned bamboo tightly wrapped in a casing of coir rope with a capacious turban of cloth bulging at its bottom end. The coconut scraper (hiramaney) was a short stool about four inches from the ground. Its seat was shaped like a violin to accommodate the cook's bottom as she sat sideways and scraped coconut halves against a circular saw-toothed metal scraper mounted on a curved stem like the neck of an angry goose. Modernity infiltrated the old kitchen in the shape of the meat-mincer clamped on to the kitchen table. Red meat, stored in a mesh fronted "meat safe", hopefully rat proof, was not yet a forbidden substance. There was no shortage of volunteers, among us children, to turn the mincer handle and watch gobbets of meat transformed into earthworm-like ribbons or granules en route to becoming tasty cutlets and patties. In hindsight one now realizes that the food we ate was "organic" (in today's jargon) and truly homemade – in that it was chopped, pounded, ground and minced – all by the bone-weary hands of the kussi ammas of old.

Bitter Medicine

Old scars in my knees yet wince when I recall the excruciating pain involved in healing the gashes and bruises of childhood falls. As soon as the blood was washed off, teeth were ground to bear the hideous bite of iodine liberally daubed while the victim screamed "Smarting!" Minor scrapes were painted with the exotic sounding Friar's Balsam, strangely sweet smelling yet with a bite. Festering was routine and the wound was thoroughly (i.e. brutally) cleaned after which a square of lint, powdered with Boric, was bandaged on. Every morning the adhering lint was soaked in hotwater and tweaked off to childhood shrieks. The "All clear" came after many days - until the next fall.

The "opening dose" was a therapeutic torture Mother firmly believed in. Once a month we were dosed while being given the condemned man's choice of the noose or the electric chair i.e. horribly thick castor oil or unspeakably bitter Epsom salts. It is amazing our guts survived this brutal irrigation.

Coughs, rashes, stomach aches meant a short walk up Horseshoe Street to Dr. Daniel de Silva's dispensary round the corner on Trincomalee Street. I seem to remember the entrance flanked by two showcases sporting huge bulbous glass bottles – one red, one blue. Dr. Dainel was a treasured family friend and he got me to stick out the tongue and applied the stethoscope while chatting away. There were no chemists, druggists or pharmacies such as proliferate today. Every doctor's dispensary lived up to its name. One carried the scribbled prescription down to Dr. Daniel's own dispenser who presided over a dim grotto of wonders barricaded behind tall shelves packed with strangely labelled bottles of all sizes, shapes and colours. The dispenser then got to work interpreting the prescription's short-hand. "Mixture" was an absolutely accurate description as our medicine was a mix of the contents of various large bottles. The liquid contents – coloured jade green, yellow or crimson – were poured into square shouldered bottles with incised lines each indicating one dose. As to taste – they were bitter, awful or revolting. Once the label of instructions was pasted the bottle was corked and neatly wrapped in white paper and sealed with red wax. We had great fun melting the sealing wax in the flame of a wick floating on a little raft of cork and tin in a chinaware bowl. Ointments were mashed and mixed in a ceramic mortar and then carefully spooned into little round boxes of ola leaf (or so it seemed).

Bouts of flu earned us visits from Dr. Daniel who sauntered down the street to our home dapper in white drill suit, black bag in hand and cigarette insouciantly dangling on his lips. After probing his young patients with thermometer and stethoscope he carefully washed his hands in an enamel basin placed on a stool. (Fitted wash basins with faucets in attached bathrooms were a wonder yet to come.) In addition to the standard, awful tasting, flu mixture the prescribed treatment was liquids (barley, Marmite, cunjee) for a few days. What made this dreary regime worthwhile was the thought of the time-honoured first post-flu meal – red rice, kiri hodi and pol sambol (laced with maldive fish, of course). A great and wonderful man was Dr. Daniel – he saved my life, but that is another story.

Battered Buttons

Rummaging in the old family wardrobe the other day, I came across in a concealed drawer a handful of curious little wooden artefacts. It took me some time to identify these little dumb-bell shaped objects for what they were – the wooden studs that looped button hole to button hole and kept our schoolboy shorts from gaping rudely open. Zip fasteners were rarely seen, and never on clothes. These studs seem to have evolved as a pre-emptive strike against the bashing our clothes underwent at our dhoby's sturdy arms on the rocks by the river bank at Katugastota. Sewn on buttons, as in shirts, rarely came out whole

Grandly dressed ladies on their knees

and Mother was endlessly sewing new buttons on. Coats too were equipped with button holes into which buttons of carved coconut shell or brass were threaded after dhoby laundering.

Our dhoby turned a practised deaf ear to the familiar litany of complaints of battered buttons and as he unfolded his huge bundle of crisply starched and bluey white clothes and linen. These were checked against a "dhoby-book", generally a used exercise book, where all items of clothing and household linen were neatly itemised. After the laundered clothes were packed away the week's dirty linen – and there was plenty of that from a family of four school children – was gathered into neat little piles by categories (shorts, shirts, uniforms, pillow cases etc.). They were checked by dhoby, squatting on the floor, and double checked by Mother marooned in the centre of an impressive pool of dirty linen from the cane "dirty linen basket" – an extinct item of domestic equipment. At last dhoby left with a bulging bundle on his bike. Washing domestic linen at home was undreamt in town houses and dhoby was the mainstay of a family's sartorial presentability. Monsoon season invariably meant a "dhoby strike". This was not a description of the vigorous bashing of rocks with clothes – but rather with the dhoby's absence caused by the impossibility of drying clothes in the rain. Grubby clothes signalled this season and later, when the sun came back, "clean" clothes liberally speckled with mildew.

Although clothes were never washed at home, every home had a heavy domestic iron of curious design – though I have no recollection as to what was ironed. This iron resembled George Stephenson's first steam engine illustrated in our text books. It was made of brass and had a wide mouthed funnel pointing forward. Heated with fiercely glowing coconut shells it had a little hinged trap-door at the back – just like a steam engine. An interesting curiosity but a hot and heavy burden for the sweating "Banda" or "Jane" who hefted its unwieldy weight.

The past is a strange and distant place.

THE WAR COMES TO CROSS STREET, KANDY

One quiet night, many years later, I walked again down Cross Street and paused outside the verandah gate of our childhood home, its spikes yet buffered by the wooden bar grandfather had hammered in to protect us from impalement. Before me was our former home, redolent with the memories of shared happiness. Behind me was our friendly pavement, scene of countless adventures, its once wide vistas now sadly shrunk with the end of our childhood. Nostalgia enfolded me.

Cross Street in 1939 was a quiet backwater of a peaceful Kandy. A line of huge trees towered at the Brownrigg Street end. To us they were "aeroplane trees" exploding clouds of seeds flying on propellor-like wings which we chased to our hearts' content. Behind the trees was a mossy old wall in whose crannies Sandanam, the rickshawman, hid the hooch for his evening carousing after a gruelling day of pounding the asphalt streets with his sadly battered feet. Beyond the walls were the large and gloomy houses of British civil servants. We had little to do with the far end, towards Trincomalee Street. Our games and our feuds were restricted to the pavement of lower Cross Street. The delightfully trellised Kumarasamy home, recessed a few steps below the street and lined with tubs of dwarf bamboos, marked one boundary. The other boundary was the sinister house of the Bhais, huge bearded Afghan money lenders, of strange garb, and even stranger habits, objects of our unending curiosity.

Once in a rare while the upper street made an impact on us, as on the day the police visited "Ellen Dale", a quiet house behind shuttered windows, shooed out a motley gang of dishevelled women and hang dog men and hustled them into a police lorry before our popping schoolboy eyes. We heard the incomprehensible phrase "brothel house" spoken in whispers. Pioneers, these ladies were, in what was soon to become a flourishing cottage industry in wartime.

Cross Street was aptly named. It was a true cross roads where many ways of life mingled. St. Anthony's Cathedral overshadowed our neighbourhood and every evening its bell tolled for Angelus. As Buddhists, we were initially bemused when our Catholic playmates broke off from their games to bow their heads in prayer. This ritual later came to be legitimised, with "time off" granted to the devout. Once a year the Corpus Christi procession passed our way. Grandly dressed ladies amazed us by humbly going down on their knees, on our dusty road, in worship of the flower decked shrine of their Virgin Mary. The Burgher ladies sported a wondrous variety of head gear – 'de rigeur' before the war, for church going. Aunty Edith, our neighbour, was their hat maker. Her home fascinated us – the faceless heads on which she modelled her creations of materials rich and strange, velvet and felt, silk flowers and bright feathers, wax berries, gaudy ribbons and saucy veils. We watched enthralled as she snipped, sewed and moulded her masterpieces while happily chewing her other speciality – Turkish Delight. Identifying her hats, as they bobbed along to church, was a minor pastime of ours.

A brief distance from the church, atop steep flights of steps, across the rail tracks, the Meera Macan mosque overlooked all Kandy. It was the centre of an exotic parade. We called it the "koodu perahera" when huge, revolving pagodas trundled our street to the ululation of Islamic chants accompanied by strange drums and tambours. Even more interesting to us children was the old cannon whose roar drove the crows berserk and announced the commencement and conclusion of the fast of 'Nhombi', as we called it. Cross Street folklore was that our Afghans hung vast slabs of beef at one end of their hall while they prayed at the other till they heard the cannon's roar. No sooner was it heard than they raced to tear into the beef with bare hands and teeth.

Once, imbued with the spirit of scientific inquiry, I stealthily climbed on to the Afghans' window sill, only to be detected and rewarded with a smart clout on my ear..... Thanks to the traditional generosity of the mosque, the beggars of Kandy had become accustomed to visiting Cross Street only on Thursdays when we too perched ourselves on the verandah alongside a large basket of rice which we doled into the capacious sling bags of mendicants.

Esala Perahera

The Esala Perahera was the brightest spot in our lives on the days it flowed down Cross Street right in front of our home. We did our best to monopolise our strip of pavement by packing it with all our chairs and benches, while taking shifts to police our property and shoo off timid peasants who ventured to encroach. But their gentle persistence generally wore down our resistance and we ended up packed shoulder to shoulder alongside family parties from remote hamlets. The pre-war perahera was a delightful melange of splendour and tawdriness – a glory to recall in these days of too well drilled and too uniform excellence. The elephants' garb ranged from cloth of gold to the motley of patchwork bedspreads. The glittering crimson glory of the Maligawa tusker, atwinkle with bulbs, was delightfully counterpointed by the humble bullock cart trundling behind carrying a wheezing generator. To us children, however, the greatest fun was looking out for incontinent elephants to splash smelly fountains on tightly wedged bystanders, or slyly counting "five-footed elephants" flaunting their virility with regal casualness.

Sinhala New Year saw a great criss-crossing of brass trays loaded with kavun, kokis, nestling under lace doilies. Christmas followed a similar scenario, with the trays carrying rich cake and breudher instead. We children had splendid times – only to have our insides ritually flushed out with castor oil, a firmly entrenched health superstition of that era.

War

The War seeped into our consciousness only gradually. The battles in faraway Europe had little impact on us. "Champion" comics reassured us that Rockfist Rogan RAF was giving the Germans hell, and in the British Empire all was well. To bolster morale schoolgirls, at term end concerts, feelingly warbled "There'll always be an England".

Unconcerned about earth-shaking battles, the children of Cross Street carried on playing 'pavement cricket' – our own adaptation of the gentlemanly game. Rubber balls gradually disappeared. Stones of the right size, tightly wrapped in assorted rags, had to substitute. Occasionally, these wrappings gracefully unwound in flight giving the fielders an unconventional catch. Boundaries were scored when these 'balls' reached the opposite pavement. As we were forbidden to cross the road, the scoring batsman was also counted out. Play had to be suspended while we wound up another ball!

I am not quite sure as to what came first, in our personal encounter with the war – the British 'evacuees' or the trucks. Probably the evacuees, who had escaped from Malaya one jump ahead of the invading Japanese. Forlorn groups of these 'evacuees' as they were designated (no Britisher could ever be a refugee!) listlessly wandered the streets, broke and shabby. They were rapidly packed off to Blighty before they sullied our native image of our Colonial masters.

Odd looking yellow trucks with canvas hoods came not long after. The more savvy among us did not take long to identify them as fugitives from the battles of the North African desert. Before long they were displaced by the, now familiar, trucks in brown/green splotches of jungle camouflage. "Trucks" was the accepted usage to distinguish them from our native civilian "lorries". Kandy's narrow streets became clogged with trucks of all shapes, bren-gun carriers, station wagons (officers' cars, we called them), and the tough early jeeps – as ugly as old crocks. We stood on our pavement and gaped in wonder at the endless convoys trundling through, loaded with troops of all colours. "Hallo

George – Vee" we gestured and yelled lustily at them. The Africans were objects of fascinated horror – reputed to be cannibals recruited to chew the Japanese up. But they looked disarmingly cheerful as they waved back at us. Neat rows of cadjan thatched barracks sprouted all over the playing fields of Kandy, surrounded by barbed wire. School cricket and football became distant memories.

Trucks occasionally parked briefly down our street and soldiers got off to stretch their legs, and to be followed round by us. Off such a truck Peter Watts walked into our house and politely asked for a glass of water – and friendship blossomed. He was genuinely curious about our country and Father enjoyed telling him about it. He called on us whenever he could, and we listened fascinated to the grown ups talk and gradually understood Peter's (to us) strange accent. He spoke of his wife and home, the bitter North African campaign and life in the jungle camps here. He was enthralled by Father's story of Aiyanayaka Deviyo, guardian of the Wanni about whom Peter wrote a story for publication. After that he always placed a forked twig in a sacred tree before entering the jungles. He brought us the odd gift – Naafi chocs, an amusing survival handbook for servicemen lost in the jungle and, memorably, an outsize rain cape for me which earned me the envy of my peers. He loved to eat our food and patiently answered our curious questions whenever we interrupted his conversations with Father. Once in a while he brought along another comrade in arms to meet Father and talk about Ceylon. After many months Watts was posted to "somewhere in India" as his letters said. Before he left he entrusted Father with a biscuit tin of his diaries and stories to be posted to his wife, if he was killed. I surreptitiously read the lot - got some idea of the impact of the front-line on a sensitive, articulate man. The war ended with Watts safely back in England. He got his biscuit tin back.

The thirsty soldiers gave Aunt Edith a brilliant idea. A spare room of the Catholic Club, opposite our home, was transformed into "The Cafe". It was far from raffish in spite of its Parisian name (suggested by Father, I seem to recall) – rather a staid English-style tea room which attracted home-sick Tommies in droves. The Cafe flourished. Edith was a tornado of energy, turning out mounds of sandwiches, curry puffs and gallons of tea for ravenous Tommies sick of barrack cooking. The Catholic Club threw open its billiard room as in-house entertainment, for Edith was a pillar of the church, a motherly figure who lent a kindly ear to her soldiers. If she ever detected an intellectual, he was shepherded across the road to meet Father – the savant of Cross Street. For us, The Cafe was a treasure trove providing new items for our wartime hobbies. We avidly collected, and swapped, exotic cigarette packets – Woodbines, Sweet Caporals – and strange match boxes. Quite a change from the Elephant cigarettes and Lanka Light matches our parents used.

Other Entertainment

But there were other soldiers who sought more raffish entertainment than tea and billiards. A small group of painted ladies carried on a flourishing trade in some tenements tucked away off Brownrigg Street, not very far from our haunts. We boys slyly slipped out at dusk to watch the rendezvous at a little corner boutique – smooth faced young Tommies shifting their feet in nervous anticipation till a brightly painted professional emerged from her hide-out to lead them away in a cloud of cheap scent. The shopkeeper chased us away as soon as he saw us lurking in the shadows, intent upon our studies of human behaviour.

Once, for a few weeks, Kandy was astounded by sad groups of 'white' children and women with covered heads, shabbily dressed in rusty black, who went from house to house tearfully begging in an unknown tongue but with the universal sign language of the sadly poor. Nobody could resist their drawn, pale faces and sad dark eyes and the ladies of Kandy were generous with their charity. These refugees disappeared as suddenly as they had appeared. One rumour had it that they were Armenians rescued from a torpedoed ship. Nobody ever found out how these sad people came to be beached on the shores of the Kandy Lake, or how they vanished. It will remain one of the unsolved mysteries of World War II.

An 'aero'-plane was a rare sight over pre-war Kandy and brought us all out waving vigorously at the speck in the sky. The war made them a familiar sight and we soon became blase and rarely bothered to glance up at the little planes buzzing around the Asgiriya landing strip. The searchlights at night were another story, as they criss-crossed overhead ceaselessly searching for the enemy that never came.

Strangely enough, the Easter Sunday raid on Colombo had little direct impact on Kandy – except as a source of various yarns by friends who claimed to have been around when the bombs fell. Cross Street, however, moved rapidly into Battle of Britain postures.

An ARP warden was appointed for our street. He roamed the darkened streets at dusk, in his white tin hat, rapping on windows if a chink of light violated the black-out. Children were given air raid drills, to creep under tables when the sirens went. We began to mimic the voice of the siren till sternly ordered to stop spreading false alarms. Suddenly, I was picked to head a junior House Fire Brigade by our Warden and decorated with an outsize tin hat and an H.F.B. armband. Whenever there was an alarm I rounded up my gang of acolytes and rushed around with canvas bucket and stirrup pump – to keep our street from burning!

Sadly, for us, the war abruptly ended in 1943. We left Kandy for a new life in an obscure, distant town, far away from all military activity. The war, I must admit, was good to the children of Cross Street. Looking back today at fifty years ago, the things and people of that era now seem imbued with the quaintness of an antique age.

(1992)

OUIDA AND THE LOCKED CUPBOARD

It all began with the Japanese air raid on Colombo on Easter Sunday 1942. We lived in tranquil Kandy – totally lacking in strategic significance. Ripples of the world outside touched us only lightly and our Cross Street too had its A.R.P. warden, black-out curtains and portable siren. The raid on Colombo shook us out of our slumbers. In spite of optimistic British communiques it now became clear that the "enemy" was battering at the gates of "Fortress Ceylon". The frenzied exodus from Colombo is now the stuff of legend. It was fuelled by sheer panic and incessant Brit propaganda about Japanese atrocities.

There was no panic in Kandy but rather a slow trickling away of townsfolk back to their village homes – as they did in past centuries whenever invaders threatened the town. Shops put up their shutters. All schools closed down for an indefinite April vacation. Our family was rootless in Kandy where Father taught at Dharmaraja. Our grandparents home offered no refuge as they lived in Dehiwala, in the eye of the storm. "Relief and rehabilitation" (in today's jargon) was, however, close at hand. Our dear friends the Wimalasenas immediately invited our family (two parents, four children) to share their home in Ekiriya for the duration of the war, if need be. Soon after, we locked up our house, entrusted the key to Mr. Fernando next door, and set off on our "retreat" in some style – packed into Noel Wimalasena's silver Jaguar.

Ekiriya

Ekiriya was paradise to us town-dwelling children whose playground had been the concrete pavement on to which we stepped from our verandah. Here was a spacious house in a rambling garden with trees to climb, rocks to scramble up and even a burbling little stream to paddle in. We were soon immersed in the rhythms and rituals of Kandyan village life in April, played hide and seek in cavernous "atuvas" and watched wide-eyed the robust rustic humour of an all night performance of "Sokori".

As time wore on these pastimes began to pall for me. I am sure my boredom meant more fun for my younger siblings happily rid of my bossmanship. I sorely missed books – from home, school, bookshops and the Municipal Reading Room which I sneaked into (being underage) to relish Picture Post and the Daily Mirror with its naughty "Jane" comic strip. I foresaw a dreary series of bookless days and sought solace where I could. The only reading available was the Senior Form English texts that Father had brought along, conscientious teacher that he was, to prepare lessons and test papers. Hungering for anything in print I devoured the saga in (in "Fundamental English") of the Bargerys – a shopkeeper's family in a London suburb from whose doings flowed a series of questions and exercises in comprehension and grammar (which I naturally ignored).

"Poems of Action"

Mild mannered man though he was, Father's taste in poetry was swashbuckling and the text book he had chosen was "Poems of Action". These poems enthralled me and I often walked around the house and garden, irritating my unwitting listeners, declaiming at the top of my voice those lines that moved me most :-

"Look for me by moonlight,
Watch for me by moonlight
I'll come to thee by moonlight, though hell
should bar the way"
or
"..... we prayed the prayer of soldiers
And we cried the gathering cry

And we clasped the hands of kinsmen
And we swore to do or die !"

rousing stuff that went with a gallop –

But when all was said and done, textbooks were pretty meagre fare for an avid reader. I had even been reduced to poring over the leaflets inside Ovaltine packs printed in a variety of languages – French, Spanish, Burmese etc. and laboriously attempting to "translate" them on my own ! I longed for meatier fare – narrative, adventure, schoolboy stories. And thereby hangs this tale.

The Locked Cupboard

A whimsical hexagonal room with a steep Kandyan roof housed a writing desk and a glass-fronted cupboard which at first, did not earn a second glance from me. As time wore on and reading material ran out I decided to take a closer look at this cupboard which I presumed to be a repository of official documents. My eyes were dazzled by what I saw. Behind these glass panes jostled a rich variety of books garnered by the Wimalasena brothers for three or four decades. They ranged from fat leather bound volumes of the classics and Shakespeare through exploits of the great explorers, novels of Thomas Hardy and John Galsworthy to paper backs whose exciting titles could only be barely discerned. What a feast for a book starved adolescent ! And all in an accessible cupboard – secured by a large brass padlock.

That was the problem. Our generous hostess Mrs. Wimalasena had no idea where the key was. Her husband was back in Kandy attending to unfinished business and, incidentally, stocking up on Bear's Elephant cigarettes for Father who had been driven to smoking beedies! I impatiently awaited his return, after window shopping at the cupboard, chockfull of books, planning the books I would read and in what order. Imagine my bitter disappointment when I found he had not brought the key! Some weeks were to pass before his next visit to Kandy – weeks impatiently spent by me with my nose often wistfully pressed against the glass panes of the locked cupboard drooling over the books beyond my reach.

I reminded him with such persistence that Mr. Wimalasena had absolutely no chance of forgetting the key on his next foray into Kandy. I was bursting with impatience till the padlock clicked open and I was in Paradise. But along with the key our host brought bitter sweet tidings. The Japanese fleet had been routed, Ceylon was in no danger of invasion, Kandy was safe and – schools would reopen in a few days. This meant the end of our endless holiday.

"Under Two Flags"

I was left with a treasure chest of books but only two days before I lost them forever. I feverishly ran through the books to see what I could rush through. My eyes upon an old style paper back with a wildly adventurous cover of French Foreign Legionnaires in heroic action. It was "Under Two Flags" by a mysterious woman writer with one name – Ouida.

I don't think I'll ever forget my race against time devouring its close print (two columns per page) in the fading twilight and flickering lamplight of Ekiriya. Ouida's narrative transported me into a world of Edwardian British nobility. Dashingly handsome young Lord Arthur (?) was falsely accused of cheating (at Ascot or baccarat) and had to flee England abandoning his beautiful fiancee Lady Esmeralda (?) as well as his Commission in the Household Cavalry. He sought refuge in the legendary French Foreign Legion where no questions were asked about one's origins. While in the Legion he engaged in sundry feats of bravery against villainous sheiks, Berbers, Zouaves and "lesser breeds without the law" in North Africa. In camp he won the dog-like devotion of a young boy (really Mistinguette, a girl in disguise). On account of some villainy our hero was wrongly arraigned for treason and led before a firing squad.

Meanwhile his name had been cleared in England and the message recalling him sent to the Legion's HQ. Mistinguette volunteered to deliver the message, heart broken though she was. As she galloped up she saw her beloved hero facing the firing squad. She threw herself in front of him and caught the bullet meant for him. As our hero cradled her bloodstained body in his arms she whispered her love for him with her dying breath and he kissed her – chastely, shedding a manly tear.

I finished the book that night. Next morning we returned to Kandy, bidding a sad good bye to paradaisal Ekiriya – and the now unlocked cupboard.

Epilogue

Years later, I read of the exotic Ouida, whose extravagant life had rivalled the many highly successful romances she wrote. She had been the lover of Princes and Archdukes, Earls and Counts. She wore the most flamboyant costumes and even led around a cheetah on a leash ! Such was the woman who held me in thrall for a few unforgettable hours long ago in distant Ekiriya.

BOOKSELLERS, BURIYANI, BARBERS ....

Words are keys that open cobwebbed corridors to a place distant in time – yet so close to the heart. Booksellers, buriyani, barber saloons, 'bioscope' carts – are words that call to mind the Kandy of my boyhood in the early nineteen forties.

School Book Shops

Booksellers teemed in Kandy, or so it seemed to one young book addict. Most useful, but least interesting, were the bookshops clustered at the top and of Castle Street specialising in text books and allied paraphernalia, for now out-dated skills, such as instrument boxes, pastel crayons, pen holders and nibs (G, Relief and Ladies') – which were rapidly developed into lethal weapons by ingenious schoolboys. These shops had an invigorating whiff of crisp paper, gum and ink which we inhaled tagging along behind book-list burdened parents. Hardy perennials clogged the shelves – Longman's Copy Books, Hussey's Nature Studies , Robinson's Geography, Charawanamuttu's Speed Tests in Arithmetic (the bane of my life) progressing dully from Book I, ever upwards. More interesting were the A.L. Bright Story Readers, for "supplementary reading", which dealt decorously with the exciting adventures of Robin Hood, Ulysses, Marco Polo and Sinbad the Sailor and provided inspiration for school boy gangs and games.

Not far away, Lazarus and Kandy Medical Stores tantalisingly displayed, amidst toys and patent medicines, fat and colourful schoolboy Annuals which one longingly leafed through hoping for a birthday gift.

The Corner Book Stall

As one grew older younger siblings entered school and stretched parental budgets. New books were only for the younger ones. We learnt to forage for used texts from promoted seniors and second-hand bookstalls. Thus I found paradise, most appropriately, next to Kandy's sole undertakers, at the corner of Castle and King Street. The signboard "The Yusuf's Corner Book Stall" drew my school teacher father and me through its crooked doorway and latticed windows into a dusty treasure trove. Books galore overwhelmed us – crammed on overloaded shelves, leaning towers of books, piled on the floor, rusty tin trunks with open lids spilling the musty odour of exotic old books. Trestle tables on the pavement outside tempted schoolboys with the comics of the day – Beano, Film Fun, Champion, Triumph and Grey Friars, fascinating chronicles of Desperate Dan, Stan and Ollie, Rockfist Rogan RAF and Billy Bunter.

Mr. Yusuf was a sturdy man with an impressive handlebar moustache, in sarong and khaki tunic. I believe be collected his stock in trade from outstations at planters' clubs and school libraries. Schoolboys bartered old texts for new comics, or flogged them for the few cents needed to hire a bike for a joyride while "cutting school." I never plumbed the mystery of Yusuf's unfailing supply of wartime comics which found their way to his shelves across submarine infested seas. We were thrilled by their wondrous tales of brave Brits bashing nasty Nazis. Old Yusuf knew his books and had an unerring eye for customer tastes. Father was guided towards dusty volumes of history and travel. And also to abridged versions of the classic historical romances and adventures of his own boyhood. Thus I waded with gusto into Hereward the Wake, The Last Days of Pompeii, and tales of ship wrecks and derring-do by R.M. Ballantyne and Capt. Frederic Marryat R.N. I acquired a quaintly skewed vision of world history where underdog Saxons outwitted wily Normans, laughing cavaliers trounced gloomy Roundheads and British redcoats laid low countless hordes of lesser (blacker!) breeds! A few of these books yet adorn my shelves, stamped with Yusuf's frank , inscribed with doggerel and scribbled sketches by schoolboys of yore. No other bookshop ever stole my heart and mind as Yusuf's Corner Book Stall.

Books on Bikes

A unique band of booksellers, neatly dressed in white verti and shirt, criss-crossed Kandy on cycles, balancing towering piles of books on plank reinforced pillions. A civil breed, they cultivated their clientele and never hesitated to display their wares even on the verandahs of young bookworms of scanty means. Surprisingly well-read, their excellent sales patter recommended authors, summarized contents and unobtrusively pushed a sale or two before they repacked their stock in trade. Great purveyors they were of P.G.Wodehouse, and the William books. Once I picked out for a few cents a battered leather volume of Arctic adventure because it had been published almost a century ago. I was thrilled to personally own such an ancient book. It is yet with me, another half century later!

An unexpected mine of reading matter in wartime Kandy was imported wrapping paper. I have never discovered how bundles of American newspapers came to end up as Kandy's wrapping paper of choice. Avid schoolboy readers discovered supplements totally devoted to comic strips – a novelty to us who only had Jiggs in the "Daily News" for comic relief. These American papers enriched our vocabulary with new slang and new heroes (a hardy few yet soldiering on half a century later!) – Flash Gordon, Terry and the Pirates, Dick Tracy, Prince Valiant and the Katzenjammer Kids. We browsed among wrapping papers in shops competing to build continuous series of adventures, with gaps filled by barter. The newly discovered Ice Age Man of the Alps flashed my memory back to one amazingly prophetic yarn of a blood thirsty prehistoric villain, preserved in a glacier, resurrected by a mad scientist (who else?) to wreak mayhem in modern times. For us Colonial schoolboys this wrapping paper unwrapped for us the enticingly different American Way of Life. The world was changing .....

Buriyani

Buriyani, to us, was synonymous with The Muslim Hotel which, as an unexpected bonus, also ran a thriving book counter of Indian publications. The Illustrated Weekly of India (sadly defunct) was tremendously popular middle brow reading. It had a cross-word promising thousands of rupees in prizes. Father's fellow thinkers of the Kandy Literary Society (is it yet around, I wonder?) sharpened their wits on these puzzles but none from Ceylon ever hit the jack pot. However, the Weekly did Father proud when they published some of his writings. Brightly coloured Tamil magazines jostled dull Indian editions of English "classics": printed on coarse paper with amazingly naive illustrations. I believe, they were readers meant for industrious mechanics and drivers, keen on self-improvement, wrestling with English in Night Schools (where are they now?)

Eating out in Kandy, in that era, gave families little choice. Cafes and restaurants had not yet emerged. Nor incredibly had the Chinese in Kandy ventured into the culinary field. They yet cycled around with bulky bundles selling cloth; regularly hooted at "Cheena! booku, booku" which enraged them as they chased the culprits brandishing their yardsticks. The Queens and Suisse Hotels were incredibly posh, the haunt of white planters and memsahibs obsequiously waited on by starched waiters. This left us with The Muslim Hotel. We were ushered upstairs to the 'family rooms' entered through swing doors, loyally decorated with pictures of Mecca, Mr. Jinnah, and portly King Farouk of Egypt resplendent in wondrous medals and topped with a fez. Children could slobber and slop curry with abandon on marble topped tables pleasantly devoid of cutlery and napery save for squares of newspaper.

The buriyani was as delicious as childhood memories will ever be. But Godamba Roti was far more exciting to us children – great fun it was to unravel yards of oily material and play rude games as we ate. The major accompaniment of buriyani and roti was the dish labelled, frankly and unashamedly, as "fowl" curry. The word 'chicken', in those simple days, meant only fluffy little yellow chaps. Only a full fledged "fowl" qualified to the curried. Wattalappan, oily and incredibly sweet, rounded off the repast.

The noisy "feeds" of schoolboys were held downstairs at long tables where we competed to score records in gobbling down stringhoppers. Oblivious to this mayhem more sober patrons chewed their way sopping up curries in little saucers with roti or stringhopper and winding up with 'aanamaalu' bananas and tender packets of 'saara bulath.'

Barbers

Kandy's barber "saloons" were democratic institutions. Gents, schoolboys, little girls, labourers and loafers all sat on the same chairs to be snipped by the same scissors. "Hair dressers" had not yet appeared to cater to class distinction. All our barbers were South Indians and lavishly decorated their walls with their gods and heroes – giving us much to look at while waiting our turn. Garish prints of Gandhi, Nehru and Subhas Chandra Bose held pride of place. I learnt of the hero-assassin Bhagat Singh from the naive portrait standing hand-cuffed arrogantly before his gallows, incongruously natty in felt hat and waxed moustache. In between were plump Indian film heroines and moon faced Chinese women in cheongsams, all looking like Mme. Chiang Kai Shek.

Summoned at last we sat before a mirrored counter cluttered with the antiquated impedimenta of barbering – bottles fitted with plungers to spray scented water to tame bristly hair; jars of, now forgotten, unguents – Afghan Snow, Attar of Roses, Mikado Scent – to perfume young men promenading the Lake bund; cut throat razors and the leather straps on which they were rhythmically stropped; opaque chunks of astringent alum to invigorate shaven cheeks; and huge powder puffs to dust our bristly heads after the regulation "short crop". A faint mist of powder, soap, scent and stubble tickled nostrils while we sat draped in rather grubby sheets and the barber snipped

Barber saloon were democratic

away. At last we stood up, the sheet was dusted with a loud whoosh and a 'podian' swept away the clippings. The barber was paid 15 cents (!) and we walked out of the swing doors feeling light in the head and cool around the ears.

"Bioscope" Carts

The media blitz to advertise the latest offerings at our only cinemas, the Empire and Wembley, were the 'bioscope' carts. Two large boards with bright posters were mounted tent-fashion on a bullock cart which paraded Kandy's streets. Inside the tent a happy band of urchins drummed a lively tattoo of baila medleys on empty tins as the cart trotted along. Intermittently they flung a handful of advertising handbills which we ran behind to collect and avidly read. Their contents were the ultimate in suspense and titillation. The story was told in vivid phrases but ended abruptly with the bracketed phrase ("see the rest on the silver screen"). Parental diktat, alas, restricted our viewing to "educational" films such as Robin Hood (with Errol Flynn), Young Tom Edison (Mickey Rooney), Marco Polo (Douglas Fairbanks) and Walt Disney films. Tarzan (Johnny Weismuller) was grudgingly accepted. To my eternal regret I never did see the sequels to the handbills' exciting preludes of the 'full serials' of Flash Gordon and such intriguing Indian Films as Toofan Mail and Vanaraja Carson (starring John Cavas, Bombay's portly answer to Weismuller).

The sound of the last tattoo has long faded away and the last 'bioscope cart' has trundled away to the Great Beyond.

Musing in tranquility, half a century later, I dream of a Kandy that is gone. Ruefully, I remind myself that, while I remember that unforgettable city, the city no longer remembers me.

BEARS, PEACOCKS AND DIVINE GIRLS

A few nights ago, watching a rerun of "From Here to Eternity" with Burt Lancaster and Deborah Kerr (remember their passionate tussle in the surf?), it struck me how much smoking went on decades ago on screen and in real life. What sultry sexiness Deborah exhaled with her languidly held cigarette, and how virile was Burt as he greedily sucked at or brutally mangled a cigarette butt ! A filmstar's style in handling a cigarette was always the clue to the character he/she portrayed in those days of "innocence", long before this activity became a danger to health and, thus, a 'politically incorrect' role model for youth.

Those of us who were children before WWII grew up in homes where our fathers smoked, and the smell of cigarette smoke permeates memories of our oh-so-distant childhood. The most popular brand was Bear's Elephant cigarettes, which originally came in 'vacuum packed' tins of fifty. Children bickered for the privilege of puncturing the tin foil seal, with the little spike neatly tucked into the lid, so we could hear the hiss as the vacuum broke. I am afraid that a tin did not last very long, as I remember occasionally running to the corner 'kaday' to buy a few loose cigarettes wrapped in paper, when a tin (of 50 !) had been finished off and a new tin not yet bought. Packets came into use only when WWII demanded that tins be recycled for the 'war effort' (bullets ? Spitfires ?). Back in peace time too these tins had been recycled and reappeared in many guises. It was said to be equal to the traditional measure of a 'chundu' and was regularly used in 'kadays' to dole out rice and other grains, in those distant days when selling by weight was unheard of. We children too had fun using these tins to pour rice into the sling bags of our regular beggars on Kandy's Cross Street. Pedlars of coconut oil neatly pierced the rims of tins and skewered them with a stick handle to ladle out their pleasant smelling wares. But what we loved best was when our curd seller came around, not with large pots of the stuff, but with a load of ex-cigarette-tins each with its own little helping of curd – that we did not have to share with our siblings.

Browns and Bears

British planters abounded in and around Kandy and – thanks to smart salesmanship – most of them rode Flying Standard cars. Brown & Co., the agents, had a huge glass-fronted showroom on Trinco Street, full of gleaming cars. It also had a greasy archway from Cross Street for car repairs. The outbreak of war spelt an end to the flow of new cars. But the building was soon acquired by a new owner – the cigarette maker Thos.Bear who dismantled the plate glass windows, on A.R.P (Air Raid Precaution) directive. Behind the now planked-up frontage, Kandy's pioneer cohort of factory girls began rolling out Bear's Elephant cigarettes – no longer in tins of fifty, but in smaller packets of ten just right for the pockets of the many thousand British soldiers who flooded the barracks around town.

Father's dear friend G.P.Malalasekera was no smoker and always ribbed his friend about his tobacco addiction. In mock seriousness he assured us children that Elephant cigarettes were thus named because their main ingredient was dried elephant dung ! This was proven by Bear's factory translocating to Kandy to be closer to elephants – its main source of raw material. We half-believed this yarn and occasionally sniffed at Father's cigarettes to see whether we could detect any whiff of elephant dung. The stars never foretold that, decades later, a son of GPM would become a leading light in the successor to Bear's Elephants !

Peacocks and Others

Elephants were not the only cigarettes in circulation in Ceylon. 'Sportsman', displaying a fox hunting gent (or was it a jockey ?) in red coat, was reputed to be a light cigarette – popular among the few ladies daring enough to smoke. One of them was on our staff in Dharmaraja and the stubs left behind in the staff room ash tray provided a dizzying introduction to smoking for my more daring classmates in Standard 3. However, the cigarette that gave rise to a host of 'urban myths' was the legendary 'Peacock'. In spite of the colourful, but mild, peacock on its label, these cigarettes of black tobacco were reputed to deliver the kick of an irate ostrich. I believe it was cheaper than the other brands being originally targetted at, what used to be called, the 'chandiya' class. But its fearsome reputation soon transcended barriers of race and class. British planters soon got to love its kick and many became loyal addicts, as did some Civil Servants and company directors who, once hooked, sniffed contemptuously at other more sissy brands. They revelled in the reverse snobbery of the taste they shared with the hoi polloi. One story going the rounds was that those addicts who demanded a bigger kick from their Peacock, popped the unopened tin into boiling water and let it stew for some minutes before savouring its flavour. As always, times change and fashions alter and the taste for Peacocks also faltered. That colourful brand is now a much rarer bird.

This was an age when smoking was well integrated into the lifestyle. Gentlemen visitors were always offered cigarettes and left behind full ashtrays. Guests at weddings were served cigarettes along with cake, and children sucked away at white 'chocolate cigarettes' with brown filter tips at one end and glowing red at the other. Our grandfathers were loyal patrons of pungent black and juicy Jaffna cheroots sold in damp bundles of ten. Our generation must have been the pioneer 'passive smokers', in today's health-speak.

Father, with his yen for trying out an exotic smoke, occasionally visited the tobacconist's counter at Cargills to buy Planter's Cut tobacco for his collection of pipes, or some pipe cleaners to get rid of the tarry nicotine in them. Once in a while his eye alighted on an unusual brand and we saw, and smelt, him trying out Players' (?) 'No Name' pipe tobacco or the oval De Reszke cigarettes in an oval tin or the most glamorous black Marcovitch with gold filter-tips. The War put an end to these luxuries. But not for long. The thousands of Allied (Brits, Indian, African and Yank) soldiers, who came to camp in and around Kandy, unleashed a dizzying variety of cigarettes on local smokers. Father was in luck's way thanks to our enterprising neighbour 'Aunty' Enid who established her Cafe for soldiers opposite our home. This became a welcome source for the various brands of cigarettes her customers got from NAAFI and were passed on to Father to savour.

My younger brother had now reached the age at which he felt he had to be a collector in order not to lose face with his neighbours – Tough Cuthbert who had a fearsome collection of toy weapons and Limping Victor who had a hidden cache of stamps stealthily pilfered from his brother's album. He hit upon the bright idea of launching a collection of cigarette packets (empty) as such a variety was readily available at home and The Cafe opposite. He also picked up anything he could off the pavement on his way to school. He built up quite a collection of exotic brands. Dim memory recalls Woodbine, Sweet Caporal, Lucky Strike, Gareth, Du Maurier in their colourful packets and the coarse paper of the 'V for Victory' meant for Indian soldiers. A valued item that occasionally came our way were the long non-safety matches with a red head that could be struck off any rough surface, such as tough cowboys did in films. My brother may have had the only collection of such ephemera in Ceylon.

'Bajiri Nona' and Divine Girls

Less welcome than the strange cigarettes the war brought us was the rationing of rice and flour. When the unfamiliar word RATION first appeared in the newspapers there was a mild controversy as to whether it should be pronounced 'ray-shun' (as in 'nation') or 'rash-un' (as in 'fashion'). The latter won. Another word and a new institution that entered our lives was the 'Depot', many of which were set up to dispense rationed commodities. In the first few months, before the hitherto unknown discipline of queuing caught on, it was a free-for-all at the depot counter with everybody waving their ration books at the harassed salesman to catch his eye, get the microscopic coupons snipped off, the rice and flour first weighed and then poured into open 'mallas'. This was no chore befitting a middle class housewife and, as such, it was delegated to me (under protest, naturally) as the eldest son. I soon acquired the skills of worming myself to the front of the throng at the Castle Street Depot, opposite the Green Cafe, and also developed some rudimentary muscles carrying home the loaded ration 'mallas'.

The Colonial government, in a campaign reminiscent of the Soviet populist campaigns to enthuse the masses about unfamiliar/unpopular moves, employed a diverse army of animators (to use today's tourist speak). One of them was Darell Pieris, a bluff character with a hearty voice who had once been a swami in Hollywood – predating the Hare Krishnas by many decades. He visited schools and was 'invited', on government instructions, to lead the assembled boys in jolly sing-songs praising the Food Drive. A wishy-washy translation of his rousing Sinhala chorus would be :

"To the garden go, lift high your hoe
Dig it deep, make veggies grow !"

By far the most interesting of these propagandists was Heidi, the wife of Father's friend Pieter Keuneman the Communist – once a suspected Comintern spy but now embraced by the British as a supporter of the 'Great Patriotic War' of Comrade Stalin against the Fascists ! Heidi's job was to reorganise the ration shops into more systematic People's Depots. (In hindsight I can now see her subtle Commie hand in smuggling this revolutionary designation into a colonial set-up). Heidi was a Hungarian redhead and was a striking figure in her populist garb of red cotton saree and bare feet. Nothing unusual today, but a real sensation in colonial Ceylon – goggled at open-mouthed both by 'natives' and British planters' wives. But a most squirming experience for me, a bespectacled and gangling thirteen year old, conscripted into escorting her, as translator, from 'kaday' to 'kaday' hunting for an elusive commodity. Heidi was, true to her Continental culture, a great smoker of cigarettes. Not any cigarette, but a particularly virulent variety that gloried in the name 'Diving Girl'. Heidi the Hungarian, being 'English-challenged', insisted on calling it 'Divine Girl'! She led me up and down the streets of Kandy looking for Divine Girls whom bemused mudalalis had never heard of. After an unsuccessful safari down Brownrigg, Castle, Colombo and King Streets we struck gold. A little 'kaday' on Hill Street tucked near Marshall's Garage had a stock of the elusive girls and Heidi snapped up the lot, to the mudalali's great satisfaction. It had being moving v e r y slowly as it had proved to be far too potent even for the consumers of Peacocks. At last, I saw the Divine Girl – a young woman in a most unrevealing 'bathing costume' (as it was politely called) wearing a bathing cap and coyly seated on a diving board. The search was over. My brother had a new packet for his collection. And whenever Heidi came back to Kandy she brought along a stock of her unforgettable Divine Girls.

P.S. I have never been a smoker !

WALKING WATHSALA HOME

I detested this chore that was imposed on me by my parents, keen to help a friend. Almost thirteen years, and yet very much under their thumb, all I could do was to put on a long suffering look and grumble loud and long. To no effect, of course.

In the 1940s our home in Kandy was on Cross Street. My brother and I walked to school at Dharmaraja College in Palace Square. My sister went to Mahamaya Girls' School, by the lake, which boasted of the only school bus in town which collected its students from their homes and brought them back after school. The bus-load of chattering girls halted briefly outside our home at No.22 and beeped for my sister who jumped in, pigtails flapping and shoe straps unbuckled. I kept out of sight, but watched warily from a window upstairs.

One evening Father was visited by Mr. R. an old friend who had just been transferred to the Kachcheri in Kandy. His official bungalow was somewhere in Asgiriya – too far away and too steep a climb for the Mahamaya bus to collect just one schoolgirl, his daughter. Father came up with a solution. On his way to work, Mr. R. could leave his daughter at our home from where she could join my sister in the school bus.

But Mr. R. saw another hitch. School was over at 1.30 p.m. but he could leave office only after 5.30 p.m. and the road home was too long and deserted for a lone schoolgirl to walk back. Father solved this problem too. "Don't worry," he said and, to my stunned disbelief, I heard him say "My son Tissa will accompany Wathsala home". Mr. R. went home a happy man, leaving behind an embittered and unwilling conscript into the ranks of chivalrous knights!

Evasive Action

As far as my fellow schoolmates were concerned, girls were an embarrassment best avoided. Even when we were out with our families, those of us unlucky enough to be burdened with sisters, took great pains to escape being seen with them, by lagging far behind the family group or scooting ahead. Any boy seen in the company of a girl was rudely ragged in school. I could never share my problem with my sure-to-be-unsympathetic friends. This was my secret burden, and I had to find my own salvation.

The day it all begain I was brusquely summoned by mother to our verandah where I had a brief glimpse of a tallish girl clutching a pile of books to her chest, before I looked away and muttered a grumpy 'Hmpf' as Mother said "This is Wathsala. You must walk with her to her home in Asgiriya". To say that we set off 'together' would be twisting the meaning of that word to describe our strange progress.

Wathsala set off first and, in approved fashion, I followed some respectable yards behind. As soon as we turned the corner into Brownrigg Street and were out of sight of home, I rapidly crossed over to the opposite side of the road, alongside some government bungalows. Wathsala continued on the pavement by the side of St. Anthony's (now St. Sylvester's) – after a quick and worried backward glance to make sure I had not bolted.

Luckily for me none of my school friends lived in this part of the town, which was the haunt of Antonians and Trinitians. I was a bundle of nerves till we crossed the railtrack near the Mayor's house and took the turn left at the Mosque on the hill, when I heaved a sigh of relief that my cousins from Trinity had not been around to revel in my humiliation.

We progressed in uneasy tandem like the two parallel lines that never met, which I had just learnt about in Geometry. I pretended interest in passing trains as we walked alongside the railtrack.

In uneasy tandem

Further on, the Police playground on my left, where we flew kites on holidays, held my interest and I lingered to watch some boys kicking a ball around. I was careful enough to make sure that my unwanted companion remained in sight.

As we went along I picked up a handy stick which I wielded like the sword of Zorro to slash at the 'val sooriya' bushes lining that unkempt road. On the fringes of my vision I noticed Wathsala taking an occasional look back to assure herself that her unwilling bodyguard was yet there. At last, the garden gate of her home came into sight. No sooner had she unlatched it than I turned round and whizzed back home like a bat out of hell.

All my attempts to wriggle out of my unpleasant task and my flimsy excuses were pooh poohed by my parents to the great amusement of Wathsala's friend, my sister.

The Long March

When this task was first imposed on my unwilling self, I had no idea that it would bind me for well over an year. Every schoolday afternoon for many, many months I was fated to escort Wathsala home. Gradually, the 'evasive action' I had initiated on our first walk settled into rigid custom. We walked on opposite sides of the road, never spoke to each other and, to the casual observer, had nothing to do with each other. And so it went on, with me lagging behind to do sightseeing or chase the odd yapping pup and Wathsala warily taking an occasional look back over her shoulder to check whether I was yet around.

Meanwhile, the world around was rapidly changing and so were we. World War II was no longer a matter of interesting headlines about Rommel, Montgomery, Zhukov and Yamashita. The great victories of the last named Japanese general changed Kandy beyond recognition. The streets were briefly crowded with shabby English refugees from Malaya before they were 'exported' back to old Blighty lest they became objects of contempt to us colonial natives.

Then came the Japanese air raid on Colombo which, after original panic, imposed Air Raid Precautions, food rationing and queues. The British now prepared for the counter-attack and Mountbatten established his SEAC HQ in Peradeniya Botanic Gardens. His troops were quartered in camps on all playgrounds in town, huge convoys of camouflaged trucks swept through our once quiet streets and searchlights stabbed the night sky above the blacked-out town.

My friends and I were growing into adolescence and our attitudes to girls were undergoing a sea change. Avoidance of their company gave place to shyness in their presence, though actual contact was but a distant dream. Romance was unheard of, and any chap harbouring soft feelings towards any girl was well advised to keep it to himself. Naturally, my silent trudges with Wathsala were never confessed to my irreverent buddies.

I gradually began to notice that my silent companion was now worth more than a cursory glance. War time austerity meant goodbye to school uniforms. After their pleated and belted sobriety Wathsala's now lissome figure looked very good indeed in her well cut coloured frocks with her thick plaits in matching ribbons. The activities of British soldiers building cadjan barracks on the playground no longer held as much interest for me as they would have earlier.

I found myself watching Wathsala as she walked with her characteristic fluidity, which had meant nothing to me when our walks began so inauspiciously. Once in a while she would look back, as if checking on me, and I would drop my glance pretending to be absorbed in some stone on the road. Our eyes never met, nor did we ever speak.

Journey's End

One day Mother told me "You'll be glad to hear that the escort duty you always grumbled about will now be over. Mr. R. has now been transferred and will leave Kandy. Your afternoons will be free after today". I kept a straight face. After all, I asked myself, was there anything to be sad about?

This to-be-last time as well we set off on our parallel sides of the road right up to her home. She always went straight ahead to her doorstep as soon as I left her at the garden gate. Today, unexpectedly, she turned round. At last the parallels met. For the first, and last, time my eyes took in her heart shaped face, dimpled chin and downward smile. Bright and brimming eyes looked straight at me with shy boldness as she softly said "Thank you, Tissa, for walking me home all these days. There will never be another time. Good bye".

A gentle wave, and she was gone. I could not mumble a farewell as my heart had taken a wild leap into my throat. Sudden sadness overcame me, and strange emotions stirred my adolescent breast. The too familiar road, we would never walk again together, now shimmered in the mist of nostalgia as I pensively trudged back home.

Childhood had ended for the boy I once had been.

TRIVIA AND TRASH

As we age, the flow of people who were young when we were young starts to diminish, then runs at a very slow trickle, then dries up almost completely. As there is yet a sizable cohort of veterans around who, like me, were adolescents in the mid-years of the last century (that phrase really does make us sound dinosaurs!) I have dug into my dustbin of memories to pay tribute to the trivia and trash I read so avidly during that time long ago. I am sure, there are yet many who share my memories though not, perhaps, the deplorable taste in reading of my younger self.

Dickens vs Rockfist

Father taught English at school (Dharmaraja, Kandy) and it was inevitable that our bookshelves at home were well stocked with books that would, hopefully, build in us a taste for good literature in later life. I have to confess that, while children's stories from Shakespeare, Dickens, Walter Scott and Longfellow, did have a certain narrative interest, their long term effect was exactly the opposite of Father's lofty hopes. An over-familiarity with their story-lines and characters built up a reluctance to chew them over once again in the unabridged originals.

Several months ago I was browsing (or was it drooling?) around bookshops in the old English village of Hay-on-Wye where every shop, castle and basement is crammed with old books, when I came face-to-face with images from my distant childhood – bound copies of 'Beano' and 'Dandy' whose silly jokes, clumsy rhymes and strange characters made us helpless with laughter. After a nostalgic dip into the world of Desperate Dan and Lord Snooty I bought a copy to amuse my grandson whose current 'comic' heroes were the teenager

Strange characters, silly jokes

Power Rangers. Not only did he enjoy my old heroes, but he also discovered that Dandy and Beano were as undead as old Dracula, and were yet being published! They now have a new fan. Off and on I came across *'Tit-Bits'* a magazine of jokes for grown-ups packed with salacious cockney humour and cartoons of busty women in embarrassing situations, not quite comprehensible to me just then.

World War II had broken out, we were older and our reading tastes more bloodthirsty. Old Yusuf's Corner Bookshop in King Street rose magnificently to the occasion. It was a wonderful little place crammed full of old books packed on rickety shelves, in open boxes and racks on the pavement. Yusuf, of the fierce handle-bar moustache, could always fish out the book we needed, whether it was a school text or adventure story by R.M.Ballantyne or Captain Marryatt who had some appeal on account of their boy heroes with whom one could empathise. But his greatest attraction, to us, was as the purveyor of *'Champion'* a magazine for boys full of thrilling stories and a colourful cover of Rockfist Rogan R.A.F.

Greyfriars, Baroness Orczy and Jane

Boys' Annuals were another phenomenon that appeared in more up-market bookshops around Christmas and I longed for a generous uncle in a giving mood. They were full of stories of adventures in strange lands, on the sports field and schoolboy pranks. Even *'Champion'* published an Annual. Foremost among the fictional public schools thus immortalised was Greyfriars where schoolboy descendants of Tom Brown played practical jokes on the Head (Quelch?) the science teacher (Stinky) and fat boy Billy Bunter. A token Indian occasionally surfaced, invariably a Maharaja's son, and always nicknamed 'Inky'. It was all fun to read and we, naturally, had no compunction in identifying with the British heroes of these yarns. Years later, my guru Reggie Siriwardena introduced me to George Orwell's mordant essay on English schoolboy stories and their (to Orwell) sickening snobbery and colonial attitudes. However, having read all these while studying throughout in Buddhist schools (Dharmaraja, Anuruddha, Sivali, Ananda) I never experienced any diminution of the highly nationalist ardour these inculcated while yet revelling in the gloriously unreal adventures of British heroes.

Teenage years and senior school gave us access to the College Library and its treasures. These were, for us, not the monumentally dull tomes recommended as supplementary reading but the novels of high adventure and swashbuckling heroes that enlivened the shelves – as bait to encourage the reading habit. The most attractive of these were by two authors now lost and drowned for ever under the floodwaters of changing tastes. One was G.A.Henty whose gung-ho stories of British redcoats battling villainous natives ' (Pathans, Zulus etc.) enthralled us. And also gave us a dim (though warped) vision of exotic lands. Henty's *"From Herat to Kabul"* – whose title gave great pleasure to the many Heraths in Dharmaraja – was our introduction to Afghanistan's bloody battles. Little did we ever imagine that sixty years later these faraway places, and much more blood, would spatter newspaper headlines.

The other was Baroness Orczy who won our hearts and whose books we impatiently lined up to borrow. Hers were swashbuckling novels of the French Revolution where the heroes were always Aristos, elegant and masterly swordsmen easily outwitting clumsy revolutionary villains. Her titles were attention grabbing – *'Scarlet Pimpernel', 'Scaramouche'* and *'The Emperor's Candlesticks'* yet echo in my memory. I have a sneaky feeling that the 'Baroness' is not recorded in Debrett's Peerage or the Almanach de Gotha. It is appropriate that she remains as elusive and mysterious as Ouida whose romance of the French Foreign Legion 'Under Two Flags' enraptured me one memorable holiday in Ekiriya, where our family fled from the Japanese invasion that never came.

The Kandy Public Library was a short walk from home and I waited impatiently to reach fourteen and thus qualify for membership. But I just could not resist the temptation to furtively slip into its Reading Room and devour the yellow bound copies of England's *Daily Mirror,* many weeks old, to relish the saucy escapades of sexy Jane – perennially escaping from the villainous Capt. Reilly Foule – in her underwear!

The prowling librarian easily detected my callow schoolboy self in a roomful of pensioners, and he good-naturedly shooed me off, only to try and try again with the persistency of Robert Bruce's spider. Alas, just a few days before I reached the impatiently awaited qualifying age of fourteen, we left Kandy for ever.

Explorers and Murderers

Father loved travel books and his book shelves carried the works of modern travellers such as Peter Fleming, Freya Stark, Aurel Stein, Marco Pallis and many more. In keeping with this interest he subscribed to *'Wide World'* a monthly (?) magazine of snappily written articles by travellers and explorers illustrated with action-packed drawings of the authors in sticky situations in exotic places. From Tahiti to Timbuctoo these intrepid white chaps were dramatically drawn, wrestling anacondas in the Amazon, camel racing with Tuaregs in the Sahara or palavering with pygmies in the Congo. I revelled in these "real life" adventures, incidentally picking up a rather white-sahib-ish view of these faraway places and "lesser breeds without the law". *'Wide World'* also carried appropriate advertisements for items desired by explorers of that bygone era – mosquito boots, collapsible bathtubs(!), snake-proof gloves etc. It also had a column on what gentlemen should wear – how to knot an Ascot, what colour socks went with brown shoes, what cap to wear with plus-fours at golf – a peep-hole into an ambience very different from our own world of blue-shorted schoolboys in a tropical Colony. WW II ended the age of intrepid white travellers and nailed the coffin of *'Wide World'*. The superbly photographed but rather prosaic journalism of the American *'National Geographic Magazine'* won over the armchair travellers, titillating them with occasional exposure of the flaccid superstructure of topless Yap Islanders and Papuans. A far cry indeed from the "No sex, please, we are (British) gentlemen!" attitude of *'Wide World'*.

In those B.T.V years our craving for visuals of world events, great and trivial, was fed by British illustrated magazines. The staid *Illustrated London News* was a stodgy album of world events and a disproportionate coverage of British Royalty in an extraordinarily dated format. Its dullness held no charm. *'Picture Post'* was the foremost of these British illustrated magazines and gave us glimpses of life in Britain just emerging from the austerity of wartime years. Gossipy news and photos of now-forgotten film stars such as Diana Dors and Margaret Lockwood; tongue-in-cheek reportage of the vulgar exhibitionism of new-rich millionaires (the Dockers?), respectful coverage of the Royal family visiting bombed-out slums or, more glamorously, as Ascot races. World news was covered, during this last twilight of the Raj – Nehru greeting India's Independence, Aung San gaining power in Burma, then famous figures of the Middle East led by playboy King Farouk of Egypt and Feisal of Iraq, and rather gloating photos of sad Germans and Japanese amidst the ruins of their shattered cities. *'Illustrated'* was a similar magazine of poorer quality. Before long we realised that both these were but poor relations of the lavishly produced American *'Life'* magazine which pushed them out of circulation. But while the going was good they gave us a visual familiarity with current events and their movers and shakers.

Very different indeed was a strange genre of American magazines that briefly enjoyed considerable popularity. These were detective magazines with titles such as *'True Detective'*. They were far removed from the genteel world of Sherlock Holmes. Large in format with lurid photos of brutally mangled corpses on the cover, they claimed to give first-hand accounts of various gruesome murders in America. Stories of serial killers, axe wielding maniacs and revengeful spouses were peppered with plenty of blood curdling photos of battered skulls, dismembered limbs and weapons of the kill. Living in (as we thought) a fairly crime-free Ceylon we relished the frisson of horror we experienced in reading this ghastly stuff. These magazines were popular enough to enliven dentists' waiting rooms – hardly the most suitable place for them. They did not have a long run, probably bludgeoned to death by the emergence of TV in America whose gory visuals rendered such wordy accounts obsolete.

In this affectionate memoir of the trivia I relished in my youth, I only echo an old friend from *Alice in Wonderland* –

> "The time has come" the Walrus said
> "To speak of many things,
> Of ships, and shoes, and sealing wax,
> Of cabbages and kings."

BADULLA

A GLIMPSE INTO THE FUTURE

The year was 1948. The University awaited me in June. As I had months of waiting ahead of me, I went off to spend a holiday, up in Badulla, in the bachelor home shared by a band of Government Staff Officers. And here I kept a diary, the only time I ever did. Little did I imagine that the life-style I briefly shared here mirrored the life I would commence six years later in 1953. My diary excerpt speaks for itself.

Sunday 29 February 1948

Up early again to see S. off at the station. Went in WJ's car. Got back and slept again. Really a day of rest.

W.J.Fernando, H & I sat the whole day in the veranda reading undisturbed save for the distant "Ho, Ho" of the goiyas ploughing with buffaloes. People here - W.J, (A.C.L.G.), Lionel Fernando, (Prison Supdt.), Herbert Hewavisenti, (Land Officer), T.B.Ekanayake, (D.R.O. Yatikinda). D.R.O. will come on Monday – gone to Kandy with R.B.Ratnayake. I'm sleeping in his room these 2 days. All quite jolly. Lionel is a big talker and quite interesting.

W.J., H & I went to the pictures – the "Outlaw". I'm going with H to Palugama on Monday – returning with A.G.A. Badulla gets its papers late, the morning paper comes in the evening and the evening papers the next morning. Postponed writing this diary.

Monday 1 March 1948

Off at about 8 with H, the L.D.O in his new Ford Prefect to Palugama for a Land Kachcheri. It is about 12 miles from Nuwara Eliya on the Badulla – Nuwara Eliya road which passes Hali-Ela and Welimada. The road climbs steadily, but for a short descent from Ettampitiya, in a never ending series of S curves along the sides of several hills. On one side is a deep valley. In places there are paddy fields terraced more steeply than I have ever seen before. They are a beautiful sight with the tender green of the young plants. I'm sure the villager here is compelled by circumstances to be more industrious than his brother in the South West. The Land Kachcheri was really at – Vangiyakumbura school on a narrow winding red road about 6 miles from Palugama. The car raised clouds of dust. The road led thru really delightful patana lands sometimes going on the top of a hill. The A.G.A. Mr. Manicca Iddakadar came a bit after us. He had brought Mr. & Mrs. Patrick Perera Supdt. of Welikada Prison who were holidaying. Mr. & Mrs. P & I went to N'Eliya in H's car. We stopped at Hakgala and walked about the gardens for some time. The plants and flowers which thrive here aren't usually found elsewhere in Ceylon. Saw oak trees and an apple tree which never flowers. From a point in the gardens we could see Haputale, B'wela, Diyatalawa and the Namunukulakanda behind which is Badulla. Mr. P could not buy what she wanted at N'Eliya as the shops had closed for lunch. Only bought some vegetables. Town was empty but as a town is far superior to the mere 'kada peliya' which is Bandarawela. The very rickshawmen here are different in dress – sarongs to the ankle, coats buttoned up, mufflers, turbans – Labourers saunter about in ex-military and naval great coats. Everyone goes about in flannels, sports coats, sweaters and woollen dresses.

As for Mr. & Mrs. P and me we did not feel too cold though none of us was wearing sweaters. Ate a few vadais and returned to Palugama circuit bungalow for lunch. A.G.A, H & the Land Clerk too were there. Went back to Vangiyakumbura for the Kachcheri. Watched it for some time – the villagers were being leased land in the village expansion areas. Cost Rs.7 per acre and Rs.2 per year after that. AGA is quite proficient in Sinhalese. After some time went with the P's to the Surveyor's camp about a mile from the school. The "camp" is a neatly kept little house with flowers and vegetables. Surveyor Noble Jayatunga – his family is in Kandy has volumes of snaps of his family and some on the walls. Good artist too, some of his drawings are on the walls. His superior Mr. Harry Panabokke. Mrs. & kids were there. He says he knows father – taught for some time in Dharmaraja after his degree, 1937 or so. Tea there. Returned in A.G.A's car with the Pereras. H will stay at circuit bungalow and return on Wednesday. Passed Gurutalawa on our way back – could not see much because of the gathering dusk. Mr. Iddakadar is a simple man – unpretentious – Passing a bo-tree while driving past in the night he doffed his hat. Reached house at about 8 p.m. Slept in H's room. D.R.O was back.

Tuesday 2 March 1948

Got up late – so did everyone else. W.J and the D.R.O. went to office at about 10. Lionel went earlier. This is their daily routine. Spent my time reading Reader's Digests and the papers. Had a afternoon nap. Went for a driver with WJ in town. He invited the Dutch ex bhikku Dhammapala who is in town, for lunch tomorrow. Mr. Eka has a car but it is in the garage for repairs and the man seems to be fleecing him. Tomorrow morning I'll be going with him for an inspection.

Went with Mr. E. for inspection. Drove down with W.J. to suspension bridge a bit out of town. This led us to foot of a hill which we ascended together with the V.H. Some fine views of town can be seen from hill. After a brisk climb we came to the land in question. A villager had occupied pasture land – refused to give it up and complains that buffaloes ruin his crops. "Goda Perakadoru" type. Began a heated – abusive argument with the gamarala and followed us halfway down the hill arguing after he had been told to surrender that land and take some in the village expansion areas.

Walked to DRO's office – a building with Kandyan door – called Headman's Lodge. W.J. picked us up a bit after 11 and went along to pick up ex bhikku D. now Mr. Van. Zeist. His hair is orangeish – red, wears casual western clothes. His talk is as interesting and thought provoking as ever. He's writing a comprehensive work on Buddhism, 5 volumes – 3 are over, 4 and 5 in parts. Dinner party tonight. Originally meant for Pereras but they could not come. Invitees. Mr. & Mrs. Shelton Ratnayake, Mr. & Mrs. Cathigeser, Dr. Will Silva, Rev. Dias Abeysinghe. H returned in the evening. Lionel managed the whole show – inviting – getting crockery and cutlery and flowers and arranging them. Pre dinner conversation on spiritualism and the supernatural. No one present was psychic so nothing was done. Dinner was a success much superior to what could be expected of bachelors. Some of the party sang after dinner. Broke up at about 10.30. DRO remained at club in blissful ignorance. Returned late with winnings at cards and a yarn of Felman.

Wednesday 3 March 1948

Up not too early, and off with W.J. in his car to Ramboda on circuit. Drove up along the same road as on the Palugama day. Arrived in N'Eliya at 11.45. Ordered lunch at "Molesworth" Guest house where W.J. stays whenever he goes up there. Parked the car outside the N'Eliya park and waited in it till lunch was ready. Lunched and were off a bit after 1.00. Ramboda is about 11 mls. from N'Eliya on the Kandy road. Once N.E is passed the scenery is different. The bare scrubland and patana on the Badulla side gives way to wooded hills. The road can be seen winding and curving very far down. More tea estates in this area – with the usual queerly spelt names e.g. Labookelle etc. The flood season had caused several earthslips on this road and sections of the road too have collapsed. They are being repaired – We passed Ramboda town proper and the famous pass – which is an enormous boulder on one side and a steep precipice on the other. W.J's work in the DRO's office did not take more than 45 mts. On our return journey we went through a heavy shower of which W.J. was glad as it washed his car which needed it badly. There was no rain beyond Hakgala. Returning W.J. held forth on astrology.

Got back home at dusk and as no one else was at home W.J. drove off straight to a film – the only means of evening relaxation here and therefore frequently visited. Film was "House of Horrors" – nothing to speak of. W.J. gave me his horoscope written by a friend to read. Interesting.

Thursday 4 March 1948

The workers went to work in their usual order – Lionel round about 9.00, H. 9.30, W.J. & DRO 10.00. Their return for lunch and after work too is in the same order daily. H. first, then Lionel, then W.J. then DRO. I read most of the day – the Reader's Digest and whatever I could discover. Postponed writing the diary from the day I came. R.B. dropped in. He's in town with other DRO's for a conference with the Permanent Secy, Education. Had a nap in the afternoon. Went with W.J. to town. He invited the DROs who were in town for dinner- also some other friends. When they came Mr.E. was in top form – the life and soul of the party – singing, joking, story telling and mimicking people. His imitation of Justice R. was superb and I hear true to life. Mr.E had a friend Mr.M. who was semi-comatose – woke up to groan a few songs and soon after dinner fell asleep. He spent the night here – in Mr.E's bed, Mr.E. on a table. The rest went away including R.B. who was at Uva Hotel. I'll be going to Uraniya on the 12th with W.J. in a station wagon. R.B. will be travelling to Mahiyangana after that.

N.B. The Easter holidays the "season" when everyone who can flocks up country from the plains is called by the planters and other sundry 'suddhas' hereabouts the Black Season !!

Friday 5 March 1948

Some of the DRO's came along in the morning and took Mr.E with them to Kalmunai and Batticaloa. The rest here went to work.

I decided that my postponing of writing up the diary for the past week had better cease before I became forgetful. As the day stretched long and the stack of reading matter here ran short I finally began writing this diary before my resolution died. I wrote up the diary from Saturday to Tuesday. Also a postcard home. When the others came here my diary writing ceased.

Intended walking to the pictures for a change but a slight drizzle began so drove with W.J. "Kiss of Death" – not very impressive but better than the other two I saw here.

Saturday 6 March 1948

H. the LDO is the quietest of the lot here as the fellow is teased a lot by the others here. It gives plenty of fun. In the nights after dinner they go to a room and carry on chatting till fairly late in the night. Its quite interesting. Lionel is the "housewife" here. He balances the budget, orders the menu when visitors are here etc. The others are quite content to leave it in his capable hands. L. is a great singer especially in his bath.

Had a morning bath, a rare experience with me. Spent the morning lazing and reading. W.J., H. & Lionel went out for lunch. Lionel played in a cricket match today – on the winning side. Utilised the time the rest were at lunch to bring diary up to yesterday – great load off my mind – a troubled conscience settled. Spent the afternoon listening to W.J. who was mildly persecuting the cook's thimble sized son. As no prospect of spending the evening profitably appeared, W.J. H. and I betook ourselves to the usual refuge, the pictures. Lionel went to church where he plays a fairly important part in the activities – taking the collection etc. There was a sharp shower in the afternoon but the evening was clear so we walked to the theatre. Picture "Adventure Island". Half the time was spent in showing 5 or 6 shorts. Picture was quite short – flimsy story. Mr.E returned tonight after a good time at Kalmunai.

Life in a bachelor establishment is quite different from that in a normal household. Here there exists an element of hazard, of surprise which adds greatly to the interest. Life is unplanned and therefore quite unhurried. There is untrammelled freedom for the exercise of each one's individual tastes. Lionel said that he is attempting to retain images of the most interesting incidents of this life to recall when he is soberly married and settled down.

INTERLUDE IN COLOMBO

A REQUIEM FOR "LION HOUSE"

The death knell rang for Lion House when the University abandoned Colombo for Peradeniya in 1952 depriving this once legendary tea-shop of the undergraduate clientele who gave it life, colour and custom. As those of us who remember it , quietly limp into 'lean and slippered' old age it is amusingly appropriate that a shop selling slippers and shoes now occupies that corner at Bambalapitiya Junction where undergrads once chattered endlessly, and aimlessly, over cold cups of tea.

When my 'cohort' entered our one and only University in 1948, "Lion House" was already well rooted in undergrad lore. Oral tradition and 'Flybynight' Vittachchi's columns had infused it with an aura we looked forward to basking in. We took a few days to get to know each other, the geography and the customs of 'College' as our seniors, with inverse snobbery, called the University. We sauntered beneath the green arches of Thurstan Road and the pillared corridors leading to K.G. Hall. Seated at the cigarette scarred tables of the Tuck Shop, with pretended sophistication, we evaluated the shy little clusters of brightly sareed 'Misses' tripping along, past the tennis courts, towards the baroque splendour of the Library at Villa Venezia. Simple 'coming of age rituals' of a long lost era.

Entree

At last we felt comfortable enough, as undergrads, to visit the Lion House we had heard so much about. Cycling along Queen's Road, past the forbidding splendour of a Colonial banker's residence we were amused by the remains of a wartime poster yet embedded in the grooved bricks of the surrounding wall. "Looting will be punishable by DEATH" it warned, in English, under the fond assumption that these law breakers could read their ruler's language!

Parking our bikes in the rickety wooden cycle stand in front, we stepped into Lion House at last. At first glance its ambience seemed hardly different from that of the University 'tuck'. Senior undergrads sat around linoleum topped tables in a haze of cigarette smoke talking University politics or evaluating lecturers and female talent. A few office workers were around for their tea/'bunnis'. Occasionally, bus travellers came along with their shopping "mallas" to refresh themselves while waiting for the next bus. Little gaggles of women undergrads shyly sidled in, generally accompanied by a male – who had already decided on which one was to be his lady love, but hadn't yet persuaded her to slip away from her protective convoy. But it didn't take too long for these groups to evolve into coy twosomes, murmuring with their heads close together, in a more tolerant atmosphere less likely to attract the envious glances and sly barbs than the 'tuck'.

The food at Lion House had a greater variety than the meagre fare at the University. But it was a far, far cry from 'cordon bleu'. As soon as a table was occupied the waiter, hopefully, plunked down a dish of the traditional stand-by 'menu' – buns, plantains (as bananas were yet called in that 'goday' age), 'muss paans', rolls, patties, sponge cakes and 'kimbulas'. In that era, just emerging from wartime austerity, most of us had very little spending money, most of which was spent on tea and cigarettes. However we did our best not to disappoint our hosts by munching on a few of the proffered items, duly grateful to the tradition of the house that undergrads were allowed to dawdle indefinitely at their tables talking endlessly of matters great and little.

Peering through the mists of uncertain memory, it is hard to recall what exactly we spoke of. I must confess that very few of our conversations ever dealt with matters of great import. I remember some verbal skirmishing between those of Trotskyite persuasion (generally from Royal) and their Stalinist opponents (from Ananda/Nalanda). We savoured the wise cracks and analysed the films seen at the old Majestic across the road, passing judgement on the vital statistics of long-forgotten stars such as Pier Angeli, Moira Shearer and Anouk, to name but a few. But much of our conversation was 'trivia and trash' – the rehashing of University gossip and trading of friendly insults. In retrospect, I believe that what held us together, other than those who fell willing victims to feminine charms, was our post-adolescent (we would have recoiled at the word) need for the rituals of male-bonding, moving around in a like-minded group.

Elections

Apart from the all-embracing and dominant Union Society, the University suffered from a surfeit of Societies, each representing some Faculty or Department thus giving great scope for 'post-hunters' keen to pad their CVs for the CCS viva. What a fruit salad it was! The Mela, Curia Historica, English Literary Circle, the Political, Philosophical and Dramatic Societies and the Nomads – much envied for their wide ranging excursions with ample opportunity for bacchanalian revels – and many more. Garnering of votes came, inevitably, at a price. Thus every election ended up with raucous victory celebrations at Lion House, at the victor's expense, of course. Although Lion House served no liquor, it never banned tipsy undergrads from vociferous celebration of election victories there. These were the only days when cash (the winner's!) flowed more freely and voters were treated to dinner – invariably stringhoppers, "fowl" curry with wattalappan for dessert.

Dinner was followed by a stampede to the Majestic, across the road, for the late show. The management quailed before the onslaught of this crowd of revellers while staid filmgoers scuttled out surrendering the hall to this horde of singing, hooting barbarians. Before we entered the hall, while the winning candidates struck a deal with the manager to pay for tickets and recompense damage, the crowd performed a frenzied war dance at whose centre was Deka Bodinagoda, in a travesty of Arab costume, belting out his signature song "Boum ! Boum ! Boum ! Abdul Hamid" with the rest of us joining in full throated chorus. The film never mattered to this audience which made rude remarks at the action, traded insults, burst into song or danced in the aisles. A tolerant Police were discreetly out of sight.

Later, unrepentant revellers limped back to Lion House to fill themselves with egg hoppers and black coffee before cycling their unsteady way back to the University hostels – Union, Brodie, Catholic, the decaying mansion "Emildalene" and even less reputable boarding houses.

The Passing Scene

Across the road was a large vacant lot (now occupied by a petrol 'shed') which was a popular location for political meetings, generally Leftist. Comrade Colvin was a great draw and whenever the tea drinkers of Lion House heard him roar, we crossed the road to swell the smallish crowd that gathered there. Those of us in the English Department smirked to ourselves to listen to Comrade Doric fulminating against the UNP government using language very, very different from the unsullied English of Tennyson and Pope on which he had lectured to us a few short hours earlier. In retrospect, it is interesting that much of this oratory was in English – and we accepted this as perfectly normal !

Beyond this open lot lay a rather dilapidated building which housed the Twentieth Century Club, reputed as the chosen venue where the sharpest intellects of the LSSP honed their wits at bridge. I seem to remember that this building, or another quite close by, carried a signboard announcing itself as the "National Institute of Higher Education" – or some such high falutin title (dime a dozen today, but rare then). It was really a cram shop for aspirants to University Education and a University lecturer, who was a shareholder, had inveigled some of his young graduates to teach there. The poor chaps had laboured for months without pay. At last when they confronted their elusive one-time lecturer he soft-talked them into accepting share certificates in a maritime salvage company he had floated. It sank not long after !

Lazily watching the passing scene through Lion House's fly-blown windows we vaguely fantasised about what cars we'd buy when (there just was no question of 'if') we got our first job. The limited models then available soon made this a pointless exercise and we consoled ourselves with the time-honoured male hobby of bird watching, regretfully aware of the limited talent that thought fit to traipse the pavements of a Bambalapitiya yet devoid of classy shops. But, whizzing past occasionally was a wonderful apparition daintily balancing herself on Ceylon's very first Vespa. This voluptuous near-Gina Lollobrigida was the Italian beauty Lydia Montagna. Here I must confess we never knew her name – till, a few years later when I was working in Trincomalee, I met her father the brilliant engineer of the 'Montana Tunnel' at Kantalai. We also glimpsed a tanned 'suddah' with a Tarzan like mane of blond hair cycling along with a spear-gun slung across his back. This was the German Gerd Von Dinklage, much pursued by gentlemen of a certain inclination.

A shabby old chap we called 'Cap(t?) Silva' who prowled the pavement was reputed to be a paedophile (then an unknown word – we used something earthier). But I believe he was just a sad and lonely old guy that we in Lion House had decided to glamourise with unspeakable vice.

Then there was the Tip Top man, a strange figure in a frosty top hat and tail coat, strangely reminiscent of a well-known statue. He carried a battered suitcase from which he attempted to peddle little jars of Tip Top Tooth Powder. But Lion House's beloved star of the performing arts was 'Kukul Charlie'. As dusk fell he emerged from whatever coop he lived in and went from table to table rendering the most realistic renditions, ever, of a rooster's cry. He never went unpaid and he earned most during the victory bashes of University Societies where tipsy undergrads attempted to outcrow him – and inevitably failed.

Finis

To conclude this tribute to a shooting star that briefly sparkled across the firmament of University life may I quote Master Shakespeare:

> "Our revels now are ended. These our actors ****
> Are melted into air, into thin air ***
> And like this insubstantial pageant faded..........

****

A LETTER TOO LATE

My dear Miss D,

Isn't this how it all began? This timid opening of my first letter to you, couched in the cautious politeness that marked our first few days of acquaintance in what was, to us freshmen of 1948, that most exhilarating of all places – the University at Thurstan Road. And this, my last letter, you will never see. I am just an old man sifting through memories and you ... are dead. My heart missed a beat and my eyes briefly misted over when I read the announcement of your death in that distant land you had made your home so very long ago. Old memories gently surface as I recall an age long lost ....

The very air seemed to tingle with effervescence during our first few weeks in that magic quadrangle of K.G.Hall, College House, Tuck Shop and Villa Venezia, beneath the green arches of Thurstan Road. It was, in many ways, an age of innocence and promise. Recently released from years of class rooms, chalk dust and the condescension of school teachers, our self esteem received a tremendous boost when our professors addressed us, at lectures, as 'Mr.' or 'Miss'. The colourful parade of these Misses, free at last from the dull chrysalis of school uniforms into bright hued sarees, was a source of unending delight and temptation. They tripped along in shy little clusters of school friends, clutching new file covers to their bosoms, while world-wise seniors prowled around to snare a willing victim. We callow freshmen could hardly compete against these sophisticates, wise to the ways of the University.

It was the alphabet that first brought us, or rather seated us,

Magic corridors

together. The list of freshmen at lectures was drawn up in alphabetic order and we were requested to sit accordingly, until such time as our professors could match names and faces. We counted ourselves fortunate to be seated next to a 'Miss' whose name began with the same initial as ours. It was a heaven sent opportunity to start chatting with girls we would otherwise never have the gumption to accost as they swayed in graceful convoys along the University's pillared corridors. I was one of the lucky ones. You sat next to me at Professor Ray's Indian History lectures. As he mangled his way through our, to him, odd Ceylonese names I learnt your run-of-the-mill 'Portuguese' surname. The professor seemed vaguely puzzled when he read out your name and saw a slim Sinhala maiden in a saree instead of the Goanese girl in a frock he was conditioned to associate with this name.

And so we met. You were 'dark and comely', with the brilliant smile you briefly flashed when I first spoke to you of ..... I know not what. Probably some banality about our Professor's eccentric garb or outlandish accent which made note-taking a daunting task. The ice was now broken and we chatted inconsequentially while waiting for lectures to commence. Whatever did we speak of ? Nothing personal for sure. All we had in common seemed to be that we were both freshmen studying Indian history. And our brief chats must have been about this. You had a charmingly disconcerting habit of turning round in your seat whenever you spoke to me – as if you gave me all your attention. I was no expert in 'body language' and did not dare to presume that this meant anything other than mere politeness. I yet counted myself among those 'heart whole and fancy free', yet hopeful of catching the eye of any one of the three lovelies whom our tuck shop peers had crowned "Top Numbers of the '48 Batch". Or of one of those more buxom misses who often performed a demure can-can at evening netball, a popular spectator sport. But it wasn't to be. No green fresher could ever match the savvy of a senior with entree to various (presumably exciting) social activities.

Your elegant profile and winsome smile were not enough to earn you a top slot in the marking scheme of our peers, which was weighted heavily in favour of the 'fair and lovely'. But you did stand out in the Indian History lectures where your inbred social ease, flowing from schooling in an elite Colombo school, was in sharp contrast to the gawkiness of many of the other girls from obscure small town schools.

You showed an exceptional speed in taking down lecture notes, and this provided me with the time-honoured gambit of borrowing your notes and thus keeping our conversations on track. You surprised me with your unusually 'masculine' script and remarked on it when I returned your notes the first time. You then let slip the first snippet of personal information "I copied the handwriting of my father who, in his turn consciously imitated that of the English Principal of his school in the hills". "So did my father, but my own script is awful and slow" I confessed "which is why I borrow your notes." We quietly slipped into the habit of walking together from our lectures, chatting of our studies and little happenings, till you caught up with your waiting friends – who had observed my 'escort duty' with sly amusement. Vague imaginings of a quiet courtship began to take shape as I cycled away. Tea for two at the tuck, perhaps, and later, sitting next to each other at a DramSoc play ..... My timid imagination dared not go any further. "If we had world enough and time" .... I thought like the poet Marvell.

Then, all at once, you were nowhere to be seen. At lectures I sat next to an empty chair, and my notes fell into irretrievable arrears. Days passed by with no sign of you. As days became weeks, I felt a strange desolation – missing something that never was, but may have been. By a strange coincidence I was reading Thomas Hardy's poetry just at this time and his lament –

> "You did not come
> And marching time drew on and wore me numb ..."

seemed to speak for me.

I finally plucked up enough boldness to ask one of the sophisticated lovelies from your old school as to what kept you away. She told me that you had left, never to return. "Her mother is in poor health and can no longer tackle a family of four teen-age brothers, and run their tea estate alone as she did for many years after she had been widowed. Our friend has now to rally round and, who knows, may have to be married off sooner than we thought. A great pity – in our class, she was the keenest to enter University". I was devastated.

After a few days of gloom, I tried to convince myself that this was no tragic "End of the Affair" (a la Graham Greene) but merely the departure of a casual acquaintance. But fate took an unexpected turn as I walked down Thurstan Road with an old friend speaking of what might have been. As we drew abreast the old pillar box he said "Why don't you write to her ? If there is no response – all you have lost is a ten cent stamp. If she does .... who knows ?"

I located your address via a friendly clerk in the Registrar's Office. It was one of those old estates up in the hill country named after some Irish County. And so it all began, with the diplomatically crafted opening which begins this story. What did I write about ? No adolescent gush of sentiment for sure. Just a tinge of regret that you had 'gone missing' and a hope that you'd come back. And then on to a chatty description of life in the University, our fellow 'Indian historians', your former school friends with whom I was now quite cordial and such like stuff in, what I imagined was, a lightly amusing style. My 'message in a bottle flung into the sea' is how I described it to my friend.

The fat envelope of your reply, hoped for but never-really-expected, bowled me over. You called me by my first name and asked me to do the same in my next letter. This invitation to keep writing was a totally unexpected bonus. You were amused by, and congratulated me on, the shrewdness of the 'soft opening' of my letter. What else did you write ? I seem to remember gentle inquiries about the University amidst whose grounds you were destined never to saunter again

– though the finality of your departure was not yet quite apparent. And sharp descriptions of life on the estate, the garden you grew and the scrapes your brothers got into. You wrote with a straightforward felicity that appealed to the critical faculty now being sharpened by my English professor.

My letters were, for you, a window on the world you left behind. University life was so interesting that no exaggeration was needed. The endless aimlessness of conversations in tuck shop and Lion House, the frenetic electioneering for posts in the Union and lesser societies followed by raucous victory celebrations, the smell of grease-paint and camaraderie at the DramSoc ..... I was never short of material for my letters.

Neither of us was so naive as to let the slightest hint of emotion surface in our letters. We both knew that mere ink and paper did not a romance make. Our correspondence quietly developed into a welcome routine and we gradually began to sense the sort of individuals we were beyond pen and ink.

Meanwhile my life in the University bubbled along as usual trying, with no great success, to balance studies with the heady champagne of like-minded company. Political debate was central in that first year of Ceylon's Independence and was carried on with vigour over endless teas in the tuck-shop, at dusk on the Bambalapitiya beach and in the various Societies that flourished and canvassed our votes.

Then, out of the blue, your next letter was from Colombo where your family had moved ! You also invited me to drop in for a chat. I could hardly believe my good fortune and lost no time in cycling along to the quiet lane you now lived in. Your mother opened the door to my nervous knock and seemed surprised at the young cyclist who asked to see you. But she ushered me in civilly enough and called out to you.

You came into the living room and smilingly greeted me by name, to my pleasant surprise. No longer were you the 'Miss' in a saree whom I had known. You were just a girl casually dressed in a frock and, unlike your mother, seemed to have expected my visit. "How good of you to come. Now bring me up to date with all the Varsity gossip that you wrote in your letters." I was immediately at ease and didn't feel the time pass or take much notice of the old ayah who studied me quizzically as she brought me a cup of tea. "No, I'm afraid I won't be coming back to the Varsity at all. I've been away far too long." I was sorely disappointed as I cycled away, but cheered up when I recalled your parting words "Do come again".

I did come again, but it was a very different scenario. A smart new car was parked in the driveway and you led me into the living room where there sat a rather sedate young doctor, with tea and sandwiches by his side, who seemed slightly taken aback at my intrusion. "This is my batch mate from Indian history lectures" you introduced me "he hopes to persuade me to resume studies. But" with a wry smile "it's now far too late for that." I got the message. I sensed the doctor's embarrassment and after a brief chat I left, achingly aware that never again would I hear you speak.

A few months later I received the invitation to your wedding, addressed in your now-so-familiar script. It was held in the rather grand old house your family had reclaimed. Apart from your former schoolmates now in the University I was the only undergraduate around in this gathering of the great and the good, your kith and kin. I found myself at the receiving end of your friends' sly jokes, which showed you had spoken to them of our strange and fleeting relationship. At last, I lined up with the other guests to wish your husband and you all happiness and 'bon voyage'. As I came up to shake your hand, we both knew that this was the first, and also the last, time our hands would touch and that we would never meet again.

****

Decades have passed since then. And suddenly, the notice of your death so far away called back to my memory that brief flicker of brightness that was you, in the distant landscape of lost youth.

It is now time to end this last letter to you, adapting Thomas Hardy, once again –

"If in heaven, will you smile at me sadly, and shake your head"

TRINCOMALEE

BEGINNING .....

When I stepped into the old Dutch building of the Trincomalee Kachcheri, exactly fifty years ago on June 1st 1953, to begin work in my very first job as a District Land Officer, little did I imagine that this unique, exasperating and most human institution would hold me in thrall for most of my working life.

Glancing through old records I am amazed both at the cool formality of the appointment procedure and at the speedy service (unbelievable today) of the old G.P.O. No Minister handed over appointment letter with fawning acolytes and press photographers in attendance. The Public Service Commission posted my letter of appointment by Registered Express Post on 20 May, promptly followed by a letter from the Land Commissioner on 25 May assigning me to Trincomalee, 160 miles from home, on 1 June. The question of palavering an MP to get another station was inconceivable. My mother meticulously packed my sailor grand father's cabin trunk with loving care and gave me instructions about dhoby accounts, polishing shoes etc. I had never, ever, lived away from home on my own. Half a century (!) ago parents were much more protective, so it was with some trepidation they were launching their first born on his own trajectory. We drove up to Trinco on 31 May, made landfall at the Resthouse and looked around the town I was to call home.

Shuffling through my rag-bag of memories a few snapshots of that long ago era and a sleepy Trincomalee stand out, bright and clear.

Trincomalee

In 1953 two distinct Trincomalees lived side-by-side. One was the old town of narrow streets and winding byways, of houses crammed together with quaint low doorways and steep roofs, crowded bazaar, jostling fish market and dusty 'maidan'. Occasionally the distinctive architecture of a kovil, mosque or church stood out from the general huddle. Two unsightly corrugated iron structures 'graced' the town. One housed a lumbering old fire engine. The other was the 'Lord Nelson' Cinema named to honour the British Royal Navy which yet had a dominant presence here. A loud, asthmatically wheezing generator powered the town's flickering lights. The Resthouse beneath a spreading banyan tree was destined to be my home.

The British Royal Navy dominated the other Trincomalee. The harbour, Dockyard and Fort Frederick were exclusively theirs, except for hundreds of civilian pen-pushers and menials who docilely trooped in every morning and checked out every evening from these enclaves. RN trucks, jeeps and staff cars of naval top brass, White Ensign fluttering, whizzed through the narrow streets. Impressive battleships rode at anchor in the harbour. It was eye-opening to me to experience, at first hand, the limitations of the Independence we claimed to have won in 1948.

The Kachcheri

My first Kachcheri had many features in common with all other such institutions. To begin with, it was housed in a musty old colonial building. Its many Branches were separated by old cupboards, filing cabinets and desks piled high with files. Clerks and staff officers scribbled away to clear 'In' trays into the 'Out'. Organisationally, a Kachcheri was like a ship – one tight unit with an unquestioned captain, sharing discipline, loyalty and comradeship, especially in crises such as disasters and elections.

The head of Trinco Kachcheri was designated 'Assistant'

Government Agent, as he was nominally under the jurisdiction of the Government Agent, Eastern Province, in distant Batticaloa. He was A.R.McHeyzer a hearty Burgher ex-serviceman, always in khaki shorts. When I recall the sartorial informality that prevailed in Kachcheris right up to the mid-1970s, I do not know whether to feel sorry for, or laugh at, today's officers togged up in ties, like salesmen, tagging along behind Ministers on field visits. The next several weeks I followed the AGA on inspections, 'Division Days' and 'land kachcheries' where he dispensed justice and/or land allotments to peasants. I absorbed his commonsensical approach to problems and began to feel the good earth beneath my feet – a far cry from the cloudy abstractions of University studies which had so engaged me only a short year ago.

A Car and a Bank

Typical of the Kachcheri way of life was the purchase of my first car. A few days after I had sat at my desk I was taken under his wing by the E.O.A (Extra Office Assistant) the benevolent Mr.Amirthalingam. "Do you have a car?" he asked me. "No." "This can't go on. How can you be a D.L.O. without a car to go on circuit ? Just fill up these forms" he said producing a set of application forms for a loan to purchase a car. Filling them up I hit a snag. I had to provide a guarantor, but I had just arrived in Trinco and knew nobody anywhere closer than distant Colombo. "No problem" said Mr.A "Just wait a minute". In a jiffy he turned up with a rather cowed looking gentleman who was introduced as "Mr.Chinniah of the Police Office next door. He has agreed to stand as your guarantor". I never knew what arm-twisting Mr.A had done to conscript Mr.C, but he signed up without a murmur and slipped away, never again to be sighted by me. Not long after I was the proud owner of a spanking new car and ready to embark on my first 'circuits'. Amirthalingam and Chinniah have long since entered 'moksha' but I always remember with gratitude the unquestioning trust they reposed in my callow self.

Purchasing a car involved the opening of a bank account. And this I did with the (to me) pretty large sum of Rs.250/- at Trinco's only bank, the Bank of Ceylon. The genial Manager Mr. Munasinghe shook my hand and gave me my first cheque book, together with a snappy button down plastic cover (which, interestingly, is the only token I ever received from this institution where I have banked for fifty years !) Signing my own cheques gave me quite an adrenaline boost.

Lodgings

My first 'home from home' in Trinco was in Love Lane, Uppuveli, in a 'chummery' (that sturdy backbone of outstation bachelor life) run by Captain Albert, an ex-soldier now turned into a, not very successful, building contractor. My address caused great amusement among my University friends, and I had to assure them that I had not shacked up in Trinco's red-light area. "Love", had been a long gone British Admiral. The Captain's deteriorating "cash flow problem" brought about a corresponding deterioration in creature comforts and cuisine quality. In desperation I deserted his establishment and sought refuge at the Resthouse.

This cool old place beneath a spreading banyan was a most interesting hostelry. Over the lunch table I came to know some of the town's young lawyers and police officers – with whom I remained good friends till today, or till they passed away. Travelling salesmen with their tall tales found a ready listener in callow me. In the evenings came the M.P., a former Vanniyar (= Rate Mahatmaya) and his buddy the Urban Council Chairman, an old Trinitian, to enjoy their tipple and the non-veg cuisine, both taboo at their orthodox Hindu homes. They treated me with avuncular concern and filled me up with useful local lore. Burly Alwis, the launch magnate, occasionally deigned to spin me a seaman's yarn.

Hartal

A couple of months after I had settled down in Trinco, the 'Great Hartal of 1953' took place and even inspired some of my University friends to go on a Quixotic march, only to be tear-gassed by Police. Interestingly, not a ripple bothered the even tenor of the Kachcheri in our faraway little town where the daily newspapers arrived only late in the evening. Our information was gleaned from the stolidly Establishment 'Daily News' which predictably assured its readers (with its customary sycophancy) that the Hartal was a total flop, and published photographs of "government offices crowded with busy clerks". I cannot quite recollect how this paper handled the Prime Minister's resignation a few days after the 'flop'. I only realised the overwhelming political impact of the Hartal when I was back in Colombo on leave. It all goes to show how remote the Trinco of yore was from developments in the nation's capital.

Ferries And Launches

I was fascinated by the fact that travelling on inspections in Trincomalee District involved crossing rivers by ferries and the sea by launch. The coastline roads leading north and south of town were criss-crossed by broad rivers which had to be forded by ferries. The volume of traffic in that era did not warrant the construction of bridges. (Fifty years later these bridges yet remain a distant dream!). Driving up the ramp of a cumbersome ferry, already loaded with traders, farmers, their women and children was a delicate task in which I acquired useful skills in both man and clutch management. Occasionally we came across an old beached ferry, looking like a whale skeleton, being repaired by a team from the Government Factory in Kolonnawa. They were a jolly lot who camped there and made themselves at home, in more ways than one, as the repair was a long process lasting many weeks.

For me, the most unforgettable experience was being on a ferry as dusk fell. The only sounds were the quiet splashing of the ferryman's paddle, a tired murmur of conversation, and the haunting cry of a 'kirala' as it flew across the darkening sky where the stars began to glimmer.

Loaded with farmers' families and my car

Crossing Koddiyar Bay by launch to Mutur, Allai Colony and Seruwila was literally an overseas adventure. These rickety boats with smelly engines were loaded to the waterline with sweaty passengers, bulky merchandise and squawking poultry. It was all so familiar to me, fresh from studying Joseph Conrad on tramp steamers in the South Seas. My official status won me a perch on the cabin roof, sunburnt and windblown as the launch along in the indigo-blue sea passing towering battleships, snappy torpedo boats, the graceful bellying sails of rice cargo boats and schools of frolicsome dolphins. Once in a rare while the engine coughed to a halt in mid-sea. The launch tossed silently while the boatmen muddled around with rusty spanners and greasy rags, while the passengers watched with customary stoicism. To a giant sigh of relief the engine sputtered back to life and chugged on to our destination – the shaky pier on the vivid green waters of Mutur's mangrove swamps.

Colonization Scheme

The experience of constructing wartime barracks in the jungle left an indelible mark on peasant colonization schemes, such as Allai. Treeless expanses, arrow-straight gravel roads, dull and boxy government buildings and cottages strung out, each standing forlorn in the middle of a desolate holding. Settlers rapidly imposed a welcome disorder on this dreary uniformity. Relatives crowded in and built cosy huddles of huts on hitherto bare allotments. Government built 'commercial centres', geometrically planned on drawing boards in Colombo, were soon abandoned to stray cattle while clusters of little shops sprang up where people needed them. Colonization schemes, in real life, developed into living organisms very different from the sterile barracks planned by 'experts'.

The nerve centre of every new colonization scheme was 'The Camp'. In addition to government offices it housed, very comfortably indeed, the staff of the Irrigation and Land Development Departments responsible for irrigation and construction. It was an enclave of privilege – comfortable houses (hierarchically graded), tennis and badminton courts, club-houses and circuit bungalows. It bustled with official activity and mud-spattered jeeps by day. By dusk tennis, cards and conviviality ruled the club houses.

Gomarankadawela Village

Centuries old villages were a pleasant contrast to the new colonization schemes and I will never forget my first visit to Gomarankadawela, where I was welcomed by an aroma which, so many decades later, yet haunts my senses – compounded of cow-dung, straw, clay floors, wood-smoke, and a faint whiff of tank mud – the essence of the Vanni village.

Departure And Arrival

Six months later I was transferred out from Trincomalee to yet another Kachcheri, a pattern of movement that was to take me to eleven more such institutions. T.S.Eliot had it right for me when he said "In my beginning is my end ....." Almost twenty years later I came back to Trincomalee, with my wife and children, to spend six of the happiest years of our lives. My first Kachcheri was, thus, my last.

Half a hundred years (!) now distance me from that green youth stepping hesitantly across the threshold of his first Kachcheri, and lost beyond recall, in the mists of fading memory, is that somnolent, peaceful Trincomalee so hospitable to him.

(1.6.2003)

THE U BOAT ADVENTURE

On my first job straight out of University I was posted to Trincomalee. Off and on I remembered my sailing grandfather when I saw the harbour with its smart British warships. (This was 1953, and the British Royal Navy yet lorded it in Trinco). Not many weeks later I set off on my first 'circuit' to Mutur to inspect peasant settlements. When my colleagues said I'd have to sail there I thought it was a joke. But it wasn't. The quickest way to reach this village south of Koddiyar Bay was to travel by launch. Naively, I expected a spanking white launch like those of the R.N. that whooshed around the harbour leaving a spume of foam behind. My spirits sank when I stepped on to the ramshackle jetty and had to push my way through a milling swarm of villagers carrying unwieldy bundles and cans, as well as bleating goats and squawking fowls, in order to reach a clumsy wooden vessel which looked barely sea-worthy. The benches of the lower deck were crammed with humankind and livestock. The top deck was pleasantly open to the sun and wind but had no seats as it was the baggage space. My clerk had 'a word in the ear' of the "captain" – a disreputable looking chap in a greasy sarong – who graciously allowed me to remain on deck, shakily perched on a bag of potatoes. After some preliminaries with a spanner and a tin of kerosene the engine finally responded to the last of several pulls on the starter rope – and we were away. I did enjoy the voyage to the steady chug of the motor – the wind in my hair, the spray in my face and the timeless vision of the billowing white sails of the boats from Kinniya loaded with rice.

My 'home' in Trinco was the Resthouse in the shade of a huge old banyan tree. Apart from assorted travellers, mostly sales reps, who frequented the place, it also was a sort of club for local worthies to enjoy a quiet tipple and chat, away from domestic taboos. The genial M.P. dropped in, once in a while, to "kill his cold/cough" with the R.H.Keeper's potent cocktail of a steaming pot of 'koththamalli' liberally laced with brandy. These friendly gentlemen often conversed with the young officer just come from the big city, thus giving me interesting insights into life in that (then) quiet, forgotten, corner of Ceylon.

Lord of the Fleet

Among the regulars was Mr. Alwis, who owned the 'fleet' of launches plying from Trinco to Mutur. He was a burly man in sarong and bush-coat who generally turned up with a coterie of acolytes. I never really learnt how he acquired his 'fleet' or the enviable monopoly of the sea route to Mutur – whose only claim to fame, long ago, was as the site of the capture of Robert Knox and his fellow castaways by the soldiers of King Rajasingha of Kandy, three hundred years earlier.

One night, as short of company as I was, he joined me for dinner at my table. As we got talking he began reminiscing about his experiences on the high seas. He was a superb story-teller and he knew when he had an appreciative audience. The tale he told me that night yet echoes in my memory, more so when I see any World War II documentaries on British convoys crossing the stormy Atlantic. In me Alwis found a listener to whom he did not have to preface his story with an account of wartime naval activity. An addict of wartime stories and films I was, in theory, pretty knowledgeable.

As a young man, rather like my grandfather, Alwis on a sudden impulse had joined a merchant ship in Colombo, as a deckhand. This was in the early 1930's. He roamed the seven seas on all sorts of ships, from tramp steamers trading coconuts in the Pacific Islands to larger merchant vessels carrying cargo from the U.S. to Britain. Meanwhile war had broken out, but the first few months of the 'phoney war', as it was called, lulled merchant ships into a sense of complacency. Alwis' ship was no different. It had a Scottish captain and sailed under the

Liberian flag. The crew was largely British but it carried an underclass of Lascars, poor labourers from India doing the dirtiest jobs. Alwis, with his sailor's savvy and inborn adeptness, was classed an 'honorary Brit'. Unsuspected, 'wolf packs' of the dreaded German U.Boats were now roaming undersea determined to blow up the 'bridge of ships' across the Atlantic that was supplying Britain from neutral America. Alwis sailed on one such ship. He now tells the story as it happened.

Torpedoed!

"One fine summer morning, as our ship was just a few days sailing from England, and the crew were carrying out their usual shipboard activities, a huge explosion rocked the ship. The alarm sounded and all of us ran panic-stricken to the top-deck. Looking seaward we saw the foaming path of a torpedo heading towards us from a submarine that had surfaced not far from us. We watched helpless and hypnotised by fear as the second torpedo exploded and the ship began to list heavily. 'Man the lifeboats!' was the cry as we were already scrambling into them. We managed to launch both boats and row away as fast as we could from the sinking ship. We watched in horror as our home on the sea, and our livelihood, upended and went down in a whirlpool. We were marooned in two boats lashed together rocking helplessly, sadly watching the scraps of wreckage and patches of oil – all that remained of our fine ship.

"Our doom seemed certain when we saw the U.Boat surface and move towards our lifeboats. Its sleek black body and sinister cannon seemed to spell our fiery death. It stopped alongside, its captain appeared on the conning tower and spoke to us through a megaphone. We couldn't believe our ears when he spoke in good English 'Sorry I had to sink your ship. We had to do it because you were carrying supplies to our enemy – England. Keep rowing due east and you should reach Ireland in a few days.' One lifeboat held the white crew members and the other the poor lascars. The German captain noticed me among the whites and shouted 'Who are you?' I replied that I was from Ceylon. 'Don't worry we Germans will free your country soon. Till then, here's something to remind you of today.' He threw something at me, which I managed to grab. It was a knife in a scabbard with a packet of German cigarettes taped to it. 'Good luck!' he shouted as the U.Boat sailed away and submerged in a burst of bubbles.

We kept rowing eastward but it was cold and backbreaking work as only our boat had oars and we were towing the deadweight of the lascars' boat. One night our crew had a whispered discussion and slipped off the tow rope. As the lascars' boat began drifting helplessly ever further away they raised loud and woeful lamentation, beseeching their gods, till their cries faded away and they disappeared on the distant horizon. I yet have nightmares in which I hear their cries. The German knife became my salvation. I have no doubt my white shipmates would have flung me aboard if I had not shown my skill with it in spearing and gutting the fish that kept us alive in the burning sun and driving rain.

Rescue

"At last we were sighted by an Irish trawler who took us into a little fishing harbour. They were poor fishermen in a poor country, but they treated us well. My shipmates went back to England. But I had had enough of war. This little fishing village had never seen a 'black' man – and one who even spoke English! I became a mascot of sorts and settled down with a pretty Irish colleen to live the rest of the war years as a fisherman in neutral Ireland .... But that's another story"

He leant back dreamily in his chair, picked a cigar, drew out a knife from an inside pocket and neatly clipped his cigar end. I was curious and he let me take a closer look at his knife. The black hilt of the razor sharp dagger was surmounted with a little silver skull. The scabbard had a little red swastika. I gasped, incredulous, for I recognized the ceremonial dagger of a Nazi officer, familiar to me from wartime films.

Alwis smiled to himself as he pocketed the dagger.

VENTURE TO THE INTERIOR

Brighter far than fading memories of first love are recollections of my first field inspection ... ...

Trincomalee 1953. I had just started work as a District Land Officer in the Kachcheri under the tutelage of its Head the Asst. Govt. Agent. I accompanied him on his circuits and observed him in action – conducting Land Kachcheries, settling boundary disputes and inspecting irrigation channels. I gradually began to get the hang of things.

Outward Bound

"T.P." house inspections were an essential part of a D.L.O's duties. This was an era of generous subsidies to peasant settlers on government land. A subsidy of Rs.700/- was paid to these who built their houses according to a govt. approved Type Plan (T.P). This was a princely sum in that far-away period when a gallon of petrol cost only Rs.1! Supervisors and Overseers inspected the initial stages of construction to ensure conformation to the approved type plan. Although initial payments were made on the certificates of these officers, the final inspection had to be done by their superior, the D.L.O. This requirement was in order to ensure that a duly approved house did, in fact, exist on the allotment and was not a mere phantom presence on the ledgers.

With a slight thrill of excitement I embarked on my first solo "venture to the interior" accompanied by the Supervisor and a pile of Land Ledgers which recorded earlier payments. Our destination was

Parana Medawachchiya, an isolated village in the jungle, some miles distant from the main village of Gomarankadawala. The Supervisor was a fund of information pointing out various sights as we drove along. The legendary hot wells of Kanniya tempted me into a slight detour. Visually they were disappointing. Ramshackle shelters stood around the mossy perimeter wall of the seven wells bubbling with hot water. I sloshed barefooted through the shallow overflow to dip my hand into a well or two to test the waters, watched bemusedly by a few bathers bucketing themselves with abandon. The water was not hot enough. I was spun the hoary old yarn that "those days" it was so hot that one could boil an egg in one particular well.

Further on, a tilted signpost indicated the overgrown road to the ancient Buddhist Shrine of Vilgam Vihara by the Periyakulam Tank. This I noted for later exploration as my archaeologist father had spoken enthusiastically of its significance.

Gomarankadawela

It was a lonely drive along this road west to Anuradhapura from which we had to turn off northwards to our destination. Once we passed the last few straggling boutiques which marked the town limits we rarely saw any life on the road. Occasionally, a knot of PWD labourers could be seen at the most desirable job in the country – languidly swinging sticks topped with little curved blades to trim the long grass by the roadside while all around them lowered dark, impenetrable jungle. Their overseer lounged somnolent in the shade. A delightful study in futility. Apart from an occasional bus or lorry few vehicles crossed our path. The road was banked up and bordered by wide grassy clearings holding back the thorny jungle, brown and grey in this hot season, enlivened by an occasional sprinkle of red or yellow "rath-mal" blossoms or the gaudy brilliance of the poisonous "niyangala". Far off, above the forest's green canopy could be glimpsed the crimson and gold splash of a tall flamboyant. The road was narrow. Whenever a bus or lorry approached I gingerly edged my car on to a side where it swayed uncomfortably, buffeted by the hot wind in the wake of the passing bus.

Once we turned off the main road the jungle was no longer at arm's length but all around us. The road was narrow, pebbly and pot-holed. Huge trees towered just by the roadside and their branches twined overhead. We drove through a shadow-stippled tunnel of trees. Monkeys swinging along the branches grimaced and chattered at us. The constant hum of cicadas was background music punctuated by the trill or squawk of a bird. Occasionally a clear patch indicated a footpath leading into the wild. A shady banyan tree with a rough bench provided a traveller's rest while offerings of leafy twigs were strung along a line – seeking the protection of Aiyanayaka Deviyo, lord of the jungle. We passed a signboard indicating Rankiri Ulpotha, an ancient hot spring which I decided to explore on my return. Duty first.

The thinning of the jungle and clearer skies indicated we were now approaching Gomarankadawela. A few government buildings were on the outskirts – the dingy line rooms of PWD workers, the Village Tribunal on a hillock, the Rural Hospital embowered in flowering bougainvillea and the tin-roofed school whose children all ran out to wave madly at this strange intruder. We parked at the doorstep of the Village Headman's house proudly indicated by his blue and white signboard topped with the Royal Crown. As I stepped out I was welcomed by an aroma which many decades later, yet haunts my memory – compounded of cow-dung, straw, clay floors, wood smoke, and the faint whiff of tank mud, the essence of the Vanni village.

We were now at Gomarankadawela's very Centre. A well trodden "plaza" of clay with a few sleepy cattle, ringed by pleasant old straw roofed houses of mud brick. Old men on string beds looked on with idle curiosity and little kids stroked my dusty car or stared at me. A cluster of women passed by carrying pots of water and wet washing on their way home from the village tank. A pleasant somnolence pervaded.

Cosily huddled huts

The VH, who also had jurisdiction over Parana Medawachchiya, was to accompany us. After a cup of strong sweet tea in the cramped little office room of his house, we set off again. My heart bled for my new car when I saw the road we were to take. It was a narrow gravel road with a strip of grass in the centre separating the wheel tracks. No motor vehicle seemed to have used this road for a long, long time. Shrubs flourished right up to the road's edge and their thorny twigs played havoc with my lovingly polished car. Occasionally we crossed a roofless bullock cart carrying bags of paddy and/or passengers clinging precariously as it swayed and jolted along the ruts. As soon as we were sighted the cart was led off the road into the trees, the acme of highway courtesy, leaving the road clear for us.

Destination

Parana Medawachchiya at last, the outermost reaches of Trincomalee District. I parked the car in the school compound where a young school mistress perched on a stool was conducting a class of little tots seated on mats. The rest of the school was in a ramshackle little schoolroom with mud brick walls, crooked jungle wood pillars and rusty tin roof patched with straw. Nothing could stem the outrush of the whole student body, about twenty in all, to goggle at this visitation from outer space. They were followed by a young school master ineffectually trying to shoo them back. I apologised for disrupting his time-table and set off on my house inspections.

A little cluster of cottages huddled cosily beneath the tall kumbuk trees on the bund of the village tank. To my town-bred eyes these houses were startlingly similar to the cartoon images of African villages in Disney's animated films. They appeared to grow out of the soil. No geometric precision marred the soft undulation of their mud walls or door and window frames, delightfully awry. My Supervisor embarrassedly explained that no experienced mason baas ever came that way to help these builders. He seemed worried that I would be a stickler for the tape measure. My instinctive sympathy for these forgotten villagers taught me my second lesson as a DLO "Peasant welfare deserves a higher priority than the rule book". (The first lesson learnt on this very circuit was "A DLO should never worry about the scratches on his car"). There was only a handful of houses for final inspection and it did not take very long to certify them as ship-shape and qualified for final payment. The humility of the peasant allotteeswas embarrassing in their submissive body language and the honorific titles they bestowed on me as I stooped into their dim little cottages with my assistants and tape measure.

Our job was done. We got back to the car to find that the school had been granted a holiday and the teachers, man and wife, were expectantly looking forward to a chat with us over lunch. We regretfully declined the lunch as we had already accepted the V.H's invitation. But we had a long conversation with these exiles from their home in Gampaha. This was an era when newspapers reached Trincomalee only in the evening. Not even a crackly radio linked to a car battery was available. Occasionally their colleague in Gomarankadawela sent them some dated papers via the weekly postal peon. Their isolation was almost absolute. The young teachers relished their chat with us and the window I briefly opened to the world outside. They did not seem embittered and were dedicated to their work. We left carrying their mail to the outside world.

Chewing and Jawing

A hearty lunch awaited us at the VH' s home. We sat at an oil cloth covered table and ate off heavy blue china plates. Red rice and curries were served in basins. The cuisine was simple and very different from city fare. The vegetables were all from local chenas – pumpkin, brinjal, murunga – not the bland "up-country" up market stuff. Not much coconut was apparent in the curries. Protein was in a curry of thin little strips – too stringy and chewy to be dry fish. It was – "Dada Mas Karavala" strips of wild boar meat and venison from jungle hunts sun-dried for preservation. I only hoped I was not savouring that other local delicacy – monkey meat!

Seated on a string bed on the verandah I had a fascinating conversation with the VH and other worthies about life in Gomarankadawela, this forgotten outpost of the old Kandyan Kingdom named after a memorable sambhur hunt. The jungle was studded with ancient ruins of the old kingdoms – pillars, moonstones, sculptures – now under the protection of guardians commanded by Aiyanayaka Deviyo, elephants, bears and the all embracing wilderness. I inquired after a distant kinsman who had been an official stationed here decades ago. They remembered him very well as he had been a lovable virile youth. "Did you know that he lived with a local girl when he was here ? He was an honourable man and gave her away in marriage before he left. You may even have met the old couple as they now live in Parana Medawachchiya". It was a revelation, though not surprising, that I stowed away to repeat with due embellishment at family reunions.

The shadows were lengthening when we left for Trinco in the gathering gloom. As we passed the forlorn village cemetery, hemmed in by jungle, my Supervisor spoke of this village's fearsome reputation for sorcery and witchcraft involving, inter alia, exhuming the newly-dead for body parts and barbecuing live Kabaragoyas to extract their poisonous tears ! Though a fan of horror movies I shuddered at this close encounter with real (?) evil. It was now too late to visit the hot springs of Rankiri Ulpotha, the Golden Pond. Deeper in the woods it was the haunt of wild elephants, and I was no hero.

"Return to Station"

Back in Trinco at last, a perfunctory wash and a dash to the tin-roofed Lord Nelson cinema to dip into the frothy escapism of an Ealing Studio comedy. My fellow film-fans were British sailors and their women-folk from the Naval Dockyard and Fort Frederick yet a British enclave. Only a few miles separated the unchanging heart of the deep Vanni from the bustle and battleships of the Naval base.

A few short miles, a few short hours ... ... I had spanned two worlds and crossed the threshold into responsible adulthood.

TRAVELLING CLAIM

Year: 1953 Month: July Date: Forgotten

Particulars of Journey			Travelled		
Time of Arrival	Time of Departure	Place of Departure/ Arrival	Vehicle Number	Distances/ Miles	Amount Paid as Vehicle Hire
11 a.m.	8 a.m.	Trincomalee	EL - 2256	29	=/40 cts. per mile
6 p.m.	2 p.m.	Parana Medawachchiya- Trincomalee		29	

AN ENCOUNTER IN THE PARK

Ever since we arrived in London my little grandson had been pestering me to take him to "the Park". He had been enthralled by the bright illustrations in his favourite nursery book of a cheery young English couple taking their little son and puppy for a walk in the park where the boy swung on the swings and sailed his toy boat on the pond. Tikiri identified himself with Tom in the book and was determined to act out his hero's adventures. At last he got the chance. His parents had gone out leaving him in my hands. And so we set off for the park, Tikiri skipping excitedly along with me sedately trailing behind carrying his toy boat. The park was not too far off for his chubby little legs nor my creaky joints.

It lived up to Tikiri's expectations. There were little boy-sized swings and, best of all, a shallow pond in which other boys were sailing their boats or hopefully fishing for fish that were not there. But he had not been prepared for the roly-poly ground squirrels who cheekily begged from visitors. We bought a packet of nuts and Tikiri, yelping happily, ran round in circles tempting the squirrels to jump up for their reward. Tired out by keeping up with his antics I persuaded him to try the quieter pastime of sailing his boat in the pond. With a sigh of relief I seated myself on a park bench where I could keep an eye on him.

On the Bench

It was a quiet weekday, and most of the adults around appeared to be grandparents like me, baby-sitting their grandchildren whose parents were at work. An English looking (one could never quite say in cosmopolitan London) woman was already seated on the bench. We exchanged the faint smiles of ritual politeness and settled down to the very English custom of reading while keeping a wary eye on our charges.

From the accent of her occasional remarks to her grandson, a much sturdier boy than mine, it was clear she was English, but not painfully posh. I pulled out the 'Sunday Island' I had collected on the flight to London and was amusedly reading the doings of our politicians and social butterflies, who now seemed so unreal and irrelevant at this distance. My companion on the bench, leafing desultorily through a colourfully illustrated women's magazine, looked across at my newspaper and spoke to me. "Your paper's not from England, isn't it – though it's in English?" "You're right. It's from Sri Lanka where I come from" I said. Uncharacteristically she continued our conversation. "Isn't that the new name of the country we called Ceylon?" "Yes" I replied "though that's the name we always used in Sinhalese, our own language."

"It's strange" she said "I lived in Ceylon for a while, many years ago when I was much younger. But I've never gone back – nor even met anybody from there till I met you today. I live in a little town Kirkcaldy in Scotland and I come to London to see my daughter's family only very rarely."

Vaguely curious about my chance companion I looked at her rather more carefully. A rather thick-set woman with characteristically slightly bulging ankles, a head of short grey hair, and a chubby face smiled back at me. "Where did you live in Ceylon and what took you there?" "Oh, it was so long ago. It was in the early '50s. My father was a harbour pilot in the Royal Navy, in Trincomalee. We lived a bit out of town, in a bungalow on a road with a romantic name – Love Lane! But it was just a dusty road lined with broken down old warehouses fenced in with rusty barbed wire." She had a faraway look in her eyes as she recalled the past. My heart skipped a few beats, but I kept a straight face, as my memory raced back to 1953.

Genevieve and the Ford

My 'home' in Trincomalee was a rather lackadaisical 'chummery' in Love Lane presided over by a retired army captain, overfond of his tipple. But he was good company and fondly regarded by the local elite – lawyers, doctors, engineers, police. I was just beginning my very first job in the district Kachcheri. I found that civilians in this 'garrison town' were definitely a lesser breed. The British Royal Navy yet ran the place with just a civil nod to the resentful civilian administration. It was a gallingly Colonial setup. However, the interior with its thatched villages, little tanks and dark jungles, was unquestionably 'ours'. My work was to take me to these forgotten places and work with humble villagers.

A month into my job, I became the proud owner of a brand new Ford Prefect. My father had strongly opposed my preference for a VW Beetle that had just appeared in Colombo's showrooms. "Nobody in that god-forsaken place will ever be able to attend to any repair. But a Ford can be repaired by any wayside blacksmith with a spanner." (How true his prediction was I discovered while standing by incompetently, many a time, while a village blacksmith clanged away at repairing the Ford). But the car was yet spanking new and I drooled over it as I washed it every morning.

Some days later, my Captain came to me with a most unusual request. On a hill nearby stood a large new house nestling amidst a well tended garden. It was occupied by an English family who were civilian staff and, as such, could not occupy RN housing in the Dockyard. Our Captain paid them an occasional visit. "I say, old chap" he addressed me "you know my friends the Smiths, who live in that large house, have seen you driving off to town every morning. Mr. Smith is the Harbour Master and works irregular hours. They were wondering whether you could give a lift in the mornings to their daughter who works in an RN office in the Dockyard." I was flabbergasted. But how on earth could I disappoint the Captain or dodge the call of chivalry? "Yes, of course" I mumbled. "Righty-O!" said my friend who had been sure of my consent "She'll come tomorrow morning."

Next morning saw Miss Smith perched gingerly on a bug-infested chair in our shabby verandah. She firmly shook the hand I nervously extended when Captain introduced us, and went to get my car. She was sturdily built and almost as tall as I was. Her brownish hair was shoulder length and, and she wore a flower patterned knee-length frock (this was decades before minis). She briskly occupied the front seat by me. "This car smells new" she remarked soon after she got in. "It's only a week old" I said with mock modesty. What I imagined myself saying was that she herself had wafted into the car an exotic aroma of perfume. But the banter of flirtatious chit-chat – and to an English girl at that – was, as yet, unfamiliar terrain. "My name's Genevieve – Jenny for short. What's yours?" As soon as I said she chuckled "Didn't your Mum know that Tessa is a girl's name?" "Maybe in England, but in Ceylon Tissa has been the name of many ancient kings", I mildly retorted.

Driving Miss Jenny

We chatted inconsequentially about Trincomalee as we drove along and shared some amusement at the inappropriateness of the name of the 'Lane' on which we lived. The drive to the Kachcheri via the drop-off for Jenny at the Dockyard, settled down to routine. It earned me some envious ribbing from my colleagues in office and my lawyer companions at lunch in the Resthouse. I fobbed them off with my assertion that it was just a polite gesture to oblige Captain and his friend the Harbour Master. But I don't think they really took my protestations seriously.

Ensconced in her cocoon of British life in the enclave of RN Trinco, Jenny had never really met any Ceylonese as social equals, apart from old Captain who dropped in on her Dad to chat, over a drink, of battles long ago. That was till she met me. Jenny was most curious as to how I had been educated so that I spoke "good English" and seemed to know as much as the Walrus in 'Alice in Wonderland'. I described the many towns I had lived in and the schools I had been to, with their wondrously knowledgeable teachers who gave us a very

Anglo-centric view of the world. I spoke proudly of our University, its brilliant professors, the romance and camaraderie of my fellow undergraduates. She listened avidly.

Jenny's had been a quiet life in a little northern town in the austere, rationed, wartime England of blackouts and air-raids, quite familiar to me from contemporary novels and films such as 'Brief Encounter'. She seemed intrigued that I seemed to know so much about the England of her birth, while she knew nothing about Ceylon. As the weeks went by we spoke about our work. She had some amusing snippets of office gossip. While I described my field visits to distant, forgotten villages nestling in the wilderness, as they had for centuries. She seemed fascinated. She took me aback one day when she asked me "Can you take me with you when you go on a village visit? I'd love to see the places you describe." I hemmed and hawed, imagining the roar of laughter with which my boss would have greeted this proposition. To say nothing of the wonderment of the villagers to see a young white woman in a straw hat mincing along behind their district officer. Weakly, I said "No Jenny, I'm afraid government regulations do not allow me to take visitors on official inspections." She seemed crestfallen.

Some days later Jenny invited me home to meet her folks. It was with some trepidation I parked my car on their driveway and walked up to their bougainvillea embowered verandah. In spite of great familiarity with English life, from books and films, I had never before been in an Englishman's house. Jenny ran up to me and, to my great embarrassment, took me by my hand and led me up to her parents seated at a lace-covered tea table laden with cakes, sandwiches and tea things. "This is Tissa, Captain's friend, who is kind enough to drive me to work every morning. I've told you about the interesting work he does in faraway villages". Mr. Smith asked me a few intelligent questions about my work. He'd travelled around the harbours of Ceylon and knew more about it than his wife or daughter. While I was nibbling away at cucumber sandwiches, Mrs. Smith said "Why don't you try the lemon cake? Jenny baked it as you were coming."

In my naivety I attributed Jenny's blushes to her shyness at her mother's pride. Mrs. Smith quietly quizzed me about my job, its prospects and the likelihood of overseas assignment. Rather unusual questions from an English lady, I thought, but I gave her honest replies. As darkness fell I rose to say "Thank you for the lovely tea, and good night". Jenny walked by me up to the car as fireflies twinkled in the flower scented dusk. Her hand rested lightly on mine as she murmured "I am so happy you came. We'll meet tomorrow" – And I drove off. Though strangely moved by her unstated yearning, my instincts rebelled against so total a surrender of my emotions so early in my untested youth. It was a restless night.

Saint Andrew's Eve

"Will you be my guest at the Trinco Club on Saturday, when it will celebrate St. Andrew's Eve?" Jenny asked me a few days after our tea. Although rather nervous at the thought of hobnobbing socially with a crowd of Britishers, I couldn't brush off the gently insistent Jenny. Fortunately it was a casual occasion and I was spared from having to explain my lack of 'black tie and tails'. A blazer and University tie were acceptable. I drove up to the Smith's house where a wondrous Jenny greeted me in a crimson, bare shoulder evening dress. She swept up to me and, in a cloud of perfume, kissed me lightly on my blushing cheek. "That shocked you a bit, didn't it?" she said, eyes twinkling as she got into the car. I mumbled something inarticulate, and kept my sweating palms on the steering wheel and my eyes straight on the road while gently Jenny hummed some romantic tune.

Jenny held my hand as we climbed the steps to the Club. She was greeted by a tall RN type with a luxuriant ginger beard. "Hullo Jen! Good to see you honouring my patron saint". "O you Scotsmen!" she exclaimed. "May I introduce you to Tissa, who is a district officer here. And this is Douglas McDonald – who's Head of Supplies Department where I work". I was one of the few non-whites in the crowd. My boss was also around and I saw him glancing amusedly in my direction as I trailed behind Jenny.

Up at the bar I had a lime juice, as I wasn't a drinking man. Jenny had a sherry and seemed both amused and slightly annoyed at my sobriety. "You seem to be the only chap around who is not honouring Scotland's national drink! I didn't know you were so goody-goody."

The kilt clad band struck up some wheezing, skirling bagpipe music and the dancing began. Jenny's toes were tapping and she angrily whispered to me "Come on, man. Let's get on the floor". My man-of-the-world facade crumbled: I don't ..." I stuttered in embarrassment "I mean, I can't. I don't know to dance". Those were the days when 'dancing' meant fox-trots and waltzes painfully learnt at dance 'academies' or from girl friends. I had no inclination for either – nor any sense of rhythm. So I just could not dance. If looks could kill, Jenny's scornful look would have felled me on the spot.

But a cavalier was at hand. MacDonald gallantly stepped up to the quietly fuming Jenny. "May I?" he said and swept her off to the vigorous cavortings of Scottish reels and the like. Several dances later Jenny came up to me, flushed with excitement to where I glumly sat. "D'you mind driving back alone? Doug will take me home. Okay?" Much relieved, I agreed. "Well, thanks for everything. Good-bye".

Providentially, a few days later I received orders transferring me to the hill station of Nuwara Eliya. I never met Jenny again ...

Back on the Bench

"Come back, Tikiri," I called my grandson "that's enough for today." My companion on the bench spoke up "When I lived in Trincomalee I knew a young man whose name sounded rather like your grandson's ...." a reminiscent smile fluttered on her lips. Clutching Tikiri's pudgy hand I rose from the bench and bade Jenny, who knew me no longer, "Good-bye". This time, for ever.

ANURADHAPURA / "PURANAPURA"

MY POSON HOLIDAY

On Wednesday, the day before Poson, my father decided to take us to Anuradhapura. As we were going in the train something hard struck mother. She thought it was a stone, for she saw some boys throwing something at the train. But the guard told us it was a bag of flowers which people who can't go to Anuradhapura throw to those who go there.

We reached Anuradhapura when it was midnight. When we went to our friend's house we saw that the verandah and the compound were full of pilgrims. In the morning we went to see the Sacred Bo-tree and Ruwanweli. From time to time we saw pilgrims coming in little peraheras and heaping milk rice by the side of the Bo-tree wall. It was difficult to go near Ruwanweli because the road was full of people and open-air shops; and the shop-keepers were trying to drag us to buy their goods. The noises were enough to make you deaf. The Brazen Palace was a sad mass of pillars, and small Thuparama was shining white in the sunshine. I like Jethavana and Abayagiri which were noble because they remain ruined. Abayagiri is bigger than all the pyramids except the Great Pyramid of Gizeh. We saw many old monasteries and Tissa Weva. On a rock below its bund I saw a queer drawing. It was a circle with fishes, small circles and other signs in it. It is supposed to be the work of those who lived before the Sinhalese.

We went to Isurumuniya and saw its beautiful carvings. Then we went to Mihintale. When father was taking snaps three old upasaka-ammas came in front and refused to move. They wanted to appear in his photograph. We than saw black and lovely Kaludiya Pokuna. People said that two Kaluthimbiri trees grew on the bank, but we did not see. There were many ruins here.

After spending three grand days in Anuradhapura I returned to Kandy very glad that we got a chance to visit a ruined city.

Tissa Devendra
STD. IV A

"RAJAN"
Dharmaraja College Magazine
1939

THE GYPSY WHO STAYED

The plaintive whine of the snake-charmer's flute, as he came down our lane with his brightly dressed monkey trotting beside him, triggered my memory back almost fifty years ago when I was a callow District Land Officer in Anuradhapura Kachcheri .....

It was an old two storey building and the approach to the Land Branch was by way of a creaking wooden stairway. I was beginning to get a hang of my files as well as the people and problems that lurked within each pasteboard docket neatly titled in the copper plate script of veteran clerks. These gentlemen were my faithful trackers through the thickets of Rajarata villages and customs unfamiliar to the townsman I was. With them I walked the wooded paths to straw thatched villages and the narrow uneven bunds of abandoned little tanks and held court (Division Days in officialese) in one-roomed schools with grizzled peasants scrunched on rickety infant chairs listening to my "words of wisdom". Every week the Kachcheri had a Petition Day when villagers, from far and wide, came to keet us armed with petitions, couched in the delightfully dated English of the 'petition writer' at the Kachcheri gate. (This was 'before 1956' and English was yet the official language). They asked for land; permits for land illegally occupied; settling of boundary disputes; repair of neglected tanks and such matters. I gradually got to know a few perennial petitioners whose claims were difficult to settle and insisted on appearing almost every week. One was the distinguished Mr. B, who was the first and last man I saw wearing the once ridiculed "redda yata mahattaya" costume complete with felt hat. He kept on manfully trying to convince me that his ancestors were the rightful owners of vast extents of land which the government had grabbed and distributed to villagers. He produced bundles of fading and crumbling documents vainly expecting me to support his title and evict these villagers. He was polite, but painfully persistent, and never gave up hope that I could restore him 'his' land. Another such character was Nagoor Pitchai, the sturdy old one-legged farmer from Harakweldamana (or was it Nagadaranewa ?) whom I could identify as he hopefully stumped up the stairs on his wooden leg. He just could never understand why I could not give him all the acreage he had manfully cultivated after wresting it from the jungle.

The Gypsy

Gypsies were always around in Anuradhapura during Poson and Vesak when pilgrims flocked. Their women walked around tunelessly singing their signature song "Karuna moodey .... Naamu gileela ...." (whoever taught it to them ?) and reading the palms of hopeful young things. The men in their rakishly tied bright turbans entertained the children with their performing monkeys and their cobras dancing to the eerie wail of their flutes. As I drove out into the countryside on field visits I would occasionally overtake one of their little caravans moving to a new campsite on the outskirts of a hospitable village. A straggly line of gypsies, of all sizes, was strung out along the road accompanied by their little grey donkeys trotting along carrying furled talipot palms which were their tent-homes.

They never had anything to do with any government official and peaceably carried on their age-old way of life undisturbed by the rules and regulations that bound us less fortunate beings. I was, therefore, curious when I found a cluster of gypsies squatting together in the Kachcheri compound one Petition Day. I was more intrigued when their spokesman joined the short line of petitioners outside my room. My clerk, and adviser, a true-born son of Rajarata did not seem too happy when the old gypsy walked in nervously and bowed humbly before us to "make his submissions". He claimed that his group of gypsies had, for many years, maintained a more-or-less permanent settlement by a deserted little tank near Tambuttegama. His plea, on behalf of his tribe, was for their occupancy to be regularised by the issue of L.D.O Permits and they be permitted to cultivate paddy. My clerk was incredulous and prompted me to ask the gypsy some searching questions to establish his story. The old man stood by his story and pleaded with me to inspect their settlement. I agreed to do so – though more out of curiosity than conviction – and the gypsy seemed happy that he had found a sympathetic ear.

My clerk was politely dismissive of the whole story and amused at my gullibility. I asked him why these 'Ahikuntakas' could not be given land. He said that for centuries these 'Koothandi' (the Vanni term for gypsy) had been wanderers who lived only in temporary camps which they shifted from one village to another in an age-old cycle of travel. They never, ever, put down roots in one place as permanent settlement was abhorrent to their culture – and so was any agriculture. He told me of an old legend (remarkably like that of the Wandering Jew) where some deity had cursed the 'Koothandi' tribe never to settle permanently in any one place but to wander afield 'as long as sun and moon endure'. Curiosity was neck-to-neck with official duty when I set off to inspect the alleged settlement some weeks later.

The Encampment

Having jolted along a rutty byroad, off the main Talawa road, I saw the usual cluster of Village Headman (V.H), Overseer, petitioners and (of course) curious onlookers to lead me to 'scene of the crime'. (Note: In the Rajarata a Village Headman's Division was not called 'wasama' but 'tulana' – which irreverently reminded me of a then popular shirt branded Tulane). I headed a line of officials and villagers along a footpath bordered by thorny scrub and shaded by towering trees. Beside me walked the V.H in an ensemble now seen only in period teledramas – konday, coat and umbrella, which he kept trying to open over me (as a symbol of authority?).

At last we emerged from the forest shade into the bright sunshine of an abandoned tank bed. At one end was an encampment of talipot palm tents pitched in surprisingly orderly rows. The old gypsy who had met me in office and accompanied me to this camp now yelled out "Piyadasa!" I was intrigued as this was a clearly Sinhala name as distinct from traditional Kuravar (as gypsies called themselves) names as Vellasamy, Muttusamy. The sturdy short-haired youth who ran up looked no gypsy to me. The old man who spoke a rather quaint Sinhalese explained to me that Piyadasa was much more fluent and able to explain their problem. Meanwhile the whole encampment had been summoned by a piercing two-fingered whistle and they squatted round us in a quiet circle to listen to the exposition of their case.

Piyadasa lived up to his chief's expectations in explaining the gypsies' aspirations. Their tribe had, for countless decades, considered the area around Tambuttegama as the traditional site from which they began and ended their cycle of wandering. They had the most cordial relations with the traditional Sinhala villagers in their little settlements growing paddy below small tanks. As time went by the gypsies observed that their neighbours begain to prosper with the generous distribution of government funds to restore their tanks, build better houses and improve village roads. The gypsies met in traditional conclave, as is their custom, and the elders decided it was time for them also to have a permanent base and be entitled to some of the benefits that the government was so generous with. The environs of Tambuttegama seemed ideal. It was the traditional starting point for their annual wanderings, the neighbouring villagers were cordial and the forest around was scattered with many small abandoned tanks which could easily be restored for cultivation. Although paddy growing was not "in their blood" it was something they could easily acquire with the help of neighbouring villagers. In fact, some of them had gained experience as hired farm labourers when they wanted a break from their traditional wanderings. They were, after all, as Piyadasa stressed in his final argument, full-fledged citizens of this land from time immemorial. It was a superbly argued case.

The V.H had nothing against them except the entrenched folk-belief that Koothandi had been condemned to wander by a divine decree and that we (both gypsies and government i.e. me) were inviting the wrath of heaven if we violated it. The Cultivation Officer's objections were more practical. He doubted whether palmistry and snake-charming were skills that could be transformed into tilling the soil. The nearby villagers were, surprisingly, not averse to this experiment in social transformation. For one thing – the tank in question was comfortably distant from their own villages. Another thing was that for countless generations they had associated closely with these gypsies as seasonal neighbours and field workers. They showed none of the uneasiness that townspeople showed towards these snake-charmers and palmists. My mind was made up though I gave no such indication. With a judicious air I announced that I would make my decision known only after discussing it with the Government Agent, my chief.

The Schoolmaster's Boy

As we sat in the shade of a tree sipping warm 'oranjenbarley' I called young Piyadasa to my side and asked him how he became so fluent in Sinhalese and skilled in argument. It was an interesting story. He was a true-born gypsy – son of a snake-charmer and a palmist. While he was a little boy and his tribe was encamped somewhere near Balapitiya his mother fell seriously ill and was admitted to the local hospital where she died. Her husband and little son were with her to the end – but the tribe had moved on to fresh fields. A school-teacher's wife had also been warded in hospital at this time. She was deeply moved when she saw the distraught and helpless gypsy father and little son. Generously she offered to take over the child and look after him. She struck the gypsy as being a genuinely caring person and he handed over his son to her, promising the little boy he would visit him whenever he could.

The school teacher and her husband proved to be genuinely affectionate foster-parents who treated him as one of their own. They named him Piyadasa and educated him in the same school where both of them taught. He was a bright student and debated in the Literary Society. His father stood by his word of honour – as all gypsies are bound to do – and visited Piyadasa and his foster family twice a year in his cycle of wanderings. The father spoke to him of his people and their customs and even taught the little fellow some conjuring. The gypsy spark in him never lost its brightness in spite of the everyday world of a Southern Sinhala village school and surrounded him. Whenever he heard the plaintive 'native wood notes wild' of his father's flute Piyadasa longed to accompany him and tread the gypsy's carefree path. The school teachers were most understanding. They knew they could never keep a wildfowl caged. So they let Piyadasa go with his father when he had reached his late teens. Father and son left with love and gratitude to follow the siren song of their gypsy blood. Every year they visited the school teachers with gifts of wild honey and rare medicinal herbs – grateful tribute from their jungle home. That was how "Piyadasa" became the spokesman of the Tambuttegama gypsies.

The rest of the story is almost prosaic. The decision to settle these gypsies as 'L.D.O Allottees' was confirmed. Some weeks later I visited the now cheerful gypsies to enact the ritual of a 'Land Kachcheri' – the time-tested process of an open court at which allottees for land were selected in the presence of their peers. The gypsy traditions of respect for their elders and the resolution of conflicts in open assembly ensured a trouble free selection of – perhaps – the first ever gypsies, since time immemorial, to hold title to government land. I cannot now remember whether I had the good fortune to sign their permits before I was transferred to Nuwara Eliya, leaving behind the dark forests, little tanks and straw-thatched huts for the pine woods, hilly tracks and stone walled cottages huddled on misty mountain tops.

Time Present And Time Past

When the snake-charmer and his monkey were at our gate I invited him to entertain my grandson and granddaughter. Growing up in the sterile city they were wary of the dancing cobra but could not resist the monkey's somersaults and other tricks. When the show was over, I offered the gypsy a cup of tea, and a banana to the monkey, and asked him whether he knew the Tambuttegama gypsy settlement. His eyes lit up, as this was his home. I told him how I had been involved in its beginnings forty-five long years ago and inquired as to its present condition. It had been subsumed within the great Mahaveli Project. The gypsy settlement, however, had retained its unique identity though the old settlers had now been given larger fields, bigger houses and been redesignated 'colonists'. My friend Piyadasa was now a respected elder and responsible for insisting that all gypsy children attend school. Their age-old traditions, however, held firm. Yearly they yet hold their great conclave to settle their problems, plan their journeys to come and celebrate their marriages under the stewardship of their traditional chief. I bade him good-bye and sent him on his way with my good wishes to Piyadasa.

Looking back across the gulf of years that distances me from my youthful self, I wonder whether by my decision to settle land on the gypsies of Tambuttegama I had, unwittingly, dissolved that ancient curse condemning their tribe to roam the highways, byways and forest paths till the end of time.

THE ELEPHANT OF VAMPIRE WALAUWA

It was dusk when we reached the outskirts of Puranapura which was to be our home for the next few years. We had rented out, sight unseen, an old walauwa overlooking an ancient tank. My wife timidly hugged our baby son more closely as we entered the long, tree darkened driveway through which we caught glimpses of a tall and gloomy house. "Reminds me of Hitchcock's Psycho" she murmured. All went well, however, when we were greeted by the frail old Kumarihamy who had rented us her home and retreated to a far humbler cottage in the spacious grounds.

Vampires and Tarantulas

"Our" walauwa was embarrassingly enormous, with doorways you could ride a horse through and rooms large enough to stable an elephant. The old aristocrat who built this place had arm-twisted his Village Headmen into paying him tribute of the most valuable timber from the Rajarata jungles. Our visitors goggled at the superb teak, satin and ebony that had gone into the doors, ceilings and furniture.

As nervous young parents of a first born son we had little time for aesthetic appreciation. Our time was spent bathing baby, washing soiled nappies, rushing to the doctor for the slightest infant "ailment", combing shop-shelves for hard-to-get infant foods and sewing baby clothes. All this in addition to my work in the Kachcheri and on the field.

We soon realised that life in Puranapura involved living in the cloest proximity to a bewildering variety of fauna and insectivora who affected our life-style in many ways. Mosquitoes were the least of them and were tackled by the tried and tested mosquito nets. But there were other hazards that my city-bred wife was ill-prepared for.

Huge spiders lurked in inaccessible corners of twenty foot high ceilings. When paddy plants flowered, strange, huge flying insects, right out of the Jurassic Era, flew in to cremate themselves at the verandah lights or to be gobbled by huge mottled geckoes like little wall-crawling crocodiles. Wide eyed tree frogs, "gus gembas", hid among our clothes. Snakes of many kinds slithered into bathrooms and mega-centipedes lurked under rugs. Our nights were far from silent. The eerie howling of jackals could be heard as they hunted in the woods beyond our garden, owls hooted mournfully and clouds of bats twittered as they swooped on the carefully tended mango orchard.

And one unforgettable night we shivered to the unearthly ululation of "ulama", the devil bird whose cry foretold death. But the only deaths foretold this time was of millions of sex-mad "meru" who flew up in strange clouds from holes in the ground to fall dead in huge stinking piles beneath the street lamps after their sad, mad flight to mate with their queen.

Late one evening, in our high-ceilinged bedroom, my wife was feeding baby while I was, in customary fashion, lazily lounging in bed with a book. Occasionally, little fruit bats fluttered in and out of the wide open windows. Suddenly, my wife let out an unearthly shriek that shook me out of my reverie.

"Look! look!" she shouted and pointed a trembling finger at an enormous bat swooping around the room, with its fiercely foxy face glaring at us or so it seemed. As mother and baby huddled together in alarm I grabbed the nearest broom and went into battle waving it at the bat, hoping it would leave by the window through which it came. Bat and broom never came into contact, but our visitor tired of swooping round these timid humans, left at last. But not before it dropped a creepy little something on my bed as it whooshed off.

It was something live and was moving feebly. Armed with flashlight and stout stick I cautiously approached the creature. It was a large and hairy tarantula! Another shriek from my wife. But there was little to fear. The bat had done its worst. The tarantula was, literally, on its one last leg. The rest had gone inside the bat. It turned over and died at last and was carefully placed under a weighted glass jar – just in case....

It was fortunate that we had closed the window because we heard a soft thud as the bat attempted a return sortie to finish off its dinner. From that day on, family and friends, dubbed our home Vampire Walauwa.

The Helpful Clerk

An outstation Kachcheri always reminded me of a slightly ramshackle ship sailing the seas in fair weather and foul. It had a distinct identity, team spirit and a hierarchy humanised by camaraderie in crisis situations. Outstation towns were also friendly little places and everybody knew everybody else's domestic arrangements.

My wife and I had just established our first home and spent evenings wandering around carpentry sheds looking for basic furniture. We were, thank goodness, decades away from today's Age of Plastic.

We had been observed by Mr.G, a smart young clerk in my Land Branch. He was the son of a retired senior clerk and firmly rooted in this countryside. He had lots of local lore and I found him a pleasant and helpful companion on my field trips to remote villages during which he filled me in about Vanni culture (before the Tigers made that word an obscenity) and local gossip.

"Sir are you on the look out for a carpenter?" he asked me one day. "I know a good chap who lives not far from your home. He can't do fancy furniture but only basic items. Shall I ask him to see you?" I promptly agreed. It seemed just what we wanted and we were tired of traipsing round "vadu maduvas", whose raw wood came from illicit timber and whose owners suspected my visits as gathering information for raids.

Next evening the "vadu baas" called on us. He was an unimpressive little man with a bad limp. He was very timid and humble in addressing me as I was an officer of the Kachcheri. We were not too sure about his capabilities and we gave him a trial order of a stool. A few days later he came with the stool built so solidly that it is yet with us forty years later having withstood the onslaughts of children, grandchildren and assorted bodies.

Enter the Baas

We decided to employ Banda for our carpentry and he came to call on us one evening, with his wife and infant son, to discuss our needs. We had rarely seen such an ill-matched couple for Carlina was an exceptionally lovely woman whose beauty was not dimmed by her ragged clothes and unkempt hair. Our kitchen 'ammay' whispered to my wife that they reminded her of the ancient tale of ugly Kalagola and his beautiful wife.

Banda had a request for us. His carpentry shed was too small and too far from us for him to do our work satisfactorily. Could he have some space in our walauwa to set up a workplace and start on our furniture? We could also monitor progress? We readily agreed and allowed him the use of a spacious old garage.

My clerk Mr. G was pleased when I thanked him for introducing Banda baas to us. "He lives near my place and is a jolly good fellow," he said.

Banda settled down to a routine, once he had established working conditions to his satisfaction. There was ample space to stack the (lawfully acquired) timber as well as the work-table and tools of his trade. He came early morning and we woke up to the sounds of his sawing and hammering. Carlina brought him his lunch and

Huge and wondrous

occasionally lingered for a natter with our 'ammay' and my wife, if she had managed to put baby to sleep. Thanks to these woman-to-woman chats we learnt how this odd couple came together.

Carlina's parents were from Moratuwa, traditional homeland of carpenters. Her father Jamis had left that over-carpentered locality and ventured into the Rajarata, which had plenty of timber and hardly any carpenters. His wife and daughter, Carlina, accompanied him when he settled down in Ehetuweva, not too far from the district capital of Puranapura. As time went on Jamis took on an apprentice from the village, Nondi (lame) Banda, unimpressive, but a good carpenter. Carlina's mother died soon after and she became the housekeeper. In traditional *guru-sishya* style Jamis gave his daughter in marriage to his apprentice Banda. Not long after Jamis died of snake-bite. Banda heard the siren call of the city and moved lock, stock and barrel to a little shed on the outskirts of Puranapura. He had the skills but, alas, neither contacts nor the low-country savvy of old Jamis. Luckily for him Mr.G of the Kachcheri happened to be his neighbour. He dropped in occasionally and introduced Banda to likely customers, like us. A true friend and saviour.

The Masterpiece

Banda worked like never before and made us the furniture we required, solidly made and, off and on, embellished with an unexpected floral flourish learnt from the late Jamis. These odd curlicues made good conversation pieces when kith and kin from Colombo visited us. His masterpiece, however, was the item he built for my wife according to the rough sketch she had drawn.

She had wanted a clothes horse on which she could dry baby linen on our airy balcony. But she missed indicating the dimensions. Once the job was done Banda limped out of the garage bowed beneath the weight of a huge item of furniture, wondrous to behold. It was an enormous clothes horse to dwarf all such items ever made. It stood almost shoulder-high and was made of contrasting strips of teak, satinwood and ebony. My wife gasped in amazement and exclaimed. "This is no clothes horse it is a clothes ELEPHANT!" The name stuck and so has that bit of furniture, solid as ever, having withstood its manhandling into carts, lorries and railway bogies in the course of the numerous transfers that bedevilled us in government service. And it is a permanent reminder of the story of Banda and Carlina.

The women at home began to detect little changes in Carlina. She looked cleaner, wore better clothes and now tied a well-oiled konde, a far cry from the raggedy young woman we first met. They thought it was due to Banda's steadier income. We had allowed him the use of the old garage, and our recommendations earned him many new customers. A gentle bulge in her waistline was also noticed and remarked on favourably.

The Wheel of Change

Around this time I lost Mr.G my right-hand man and good Samaritan at the Kachcheri. In the fullness of time he earned a promotion and a transfer from the drought struck Vanni to the rain-sodden hill country. His natural alertness, intelligence and experience were sure to take him many rungs higher on the administrative ladder. I told him so as I shook his hand in regretful farewell.

One day, not long after, a distraught Banda came to see us with his sobbing little son in tow. We imagined that Carlina had suddenly been taken ill and he wanted us to put in a word to a doctor in the hospital. But his crisis was far worse. Carlina had disappeared without trace. As she had taken her meagre belongings as well, it became clear that it was a planned getaway. Who could be the villain who robbed poor Banda of his wife and happiness?

The most likely explanation lay in the 'kaday' opposite their hut, a popular stop for lorry drivers to have tea and admire the scenery. As was only to be expected, the 'kaday' man denied all knowledge. He was not going to lose customers by admitting their misdeeds, if any, to a poor carpenter. We did what we could, which was very little, to console poor Banda. He then made the bold decision to quit the town and go back home to Ehetuweva where his mother could care for his young son. It was the right decision, we assured him as he fell at our feet in tearful farewell.

A Face from the Past

Many years later we were installed in a Residency on a hill overlooking the sea. In the fullness of time I had come to head a Kachcheri. To my pleasant surprise, the first officer to greet me in my new office was Mr.G. His efficiency had earned its reward and he had been promoted to staff rank and become my deputy.

As old friends who would appreciate an informal briefing about my new Kachcheri, Mr.G invited us home for dinner. His charming convent-educated wife laid on a superb spread of 'fruit of the sea' topped off with a sophisticated dessert. When my wife complemented her on her culinary skills, she said that all credit was due to their cook Caroline who had come to her from Mr.G's mother.

When we were about to leave, my wife stepped in to the pantry to compliment the cook. To their mutual astonishment they recognized each other, but had the presence of mind to remain silent. Caroline the cook, now plump and yet attractive, was none other than Banda's run-away wife, the lovely Carlina.

Mrs.G bustled up and formally introduced the cook.

"You know she has a pretty little daughter. As G and I have no children of our own we have legally adopted her and send her to the best school in town." As we drove home to The Residency and recalled the after dinner discovery, my admiration of Mr.G's resourcefulness was boundless. What a man!

The elephant is yet with us and, apart from its legitimate function, often serves as a playhouse for our grandchildren. What a tale it would tell, if it could only talk!

BRUMPY'S DAUGHTER

Kachcheries in the 'old days' were strictly male sanctuaries. The only women workers around were garden sweepers ineffectually battling dried leaves and scraps of paper. The other women who nervously entered a Kachcheri were poor peasant petitioners to plead their cases for land, ration books, charitable allowances or divorce before a team of Staff Officers – all of them men.

When I returned to the Kachcheri at Aluth Eliya, after a few years on scholarship abroad, I found myself in a vastly changed office environment. The gates of a male fortress had been breached and sarees were everywhere – seated behind clerical desks and even within the hallowed cubicles of Staff Officers. It took some time getting used to, when a docile woman clerk came in with a file to discuss with "Sir". You had, perforce to address them as "Miss" and guard your tongue against the casual vulgarisms which peppered our discussions of problem cases with male clerks. No longer were our Staff Officers' cubicles unofficial venues for a cup of tea, a smoke, salacious gossip and raucous laughter. The 'silken invasion' of our ranks regretfully ended the age-old Kachcheri tradition of male bonding and clubby camaraderie. No longer could you stand at your cubicle door and bawl out "Perera!" or "Dissanayake!" to summon a clerk in a hurry. In the new dispensation, peons had to be despatched to request the presence of the relevant 'Miss'.

'Miss' with a Mystery

Most of our women clerks came from a rural background with a Central School education, as did most of their male colleagues.

A few were more urban and, often, daughters of fathers already in government service. In this garden of rather modest blooms which was the female cohort of Kachcheri clerks there stood out one exotic flower – the mysterious Miss Ratnayake. There was never any mystery about her competence which was of the highest level. She had the rare ability to work in Sinhala, English and Tamil. Sinhala was by now, the language of administration and our files. English remained embedded in the older strata of those long-standing files with barely soluble problems, like that of the distinguished old aristocrat who stubbornly insisted on claiming land, long since distributed to peasant farmers, based on a grant by a long dead British Governor. Tamil was the language of 'Indian' plantation workers who came to petition us on various grievances but, as most of us barely understood Tamil, were forced to communicate in 'pidgin' Sinhala.

All this changed when Miss Ratnayake came along. It was a treat to watch these humble men and women perk up and jabber away their problems to this young lady, confident in her ability to translate them to the Staff Officer who had never really understood them before this. And what is more, they felt a kinship with her as she draped her saree in Tamil style and a 'pottu' graced her brow. This was the basis of her mystery. Here was this young woman with a good Sinhala family name but dressing in the Tamil style and fluent in the language as well. Furthermore (and this was not so rare in Aluth Eliya, once home to lusty British planters) her eyes were grey and she was very fair in complexion. But ours was a tolerant town and curiosity soon faded away. It was presumed that her mother was Tamil. The fact that Miss R came to work from and lived in the local convent, legendary for its hospitality to unwanted children of embarrassing liaisons, was accepted as a reasonable explanation. 'Ratnayake' was a fiction, we thought.

Romance?

As time went by, Miss Ratnayake's exceptional competence earned her rapid promotion in the ranks and her colleagues were sure she would soon rise to Staff Officer level. But, while many of her women friends had married – either colleagues, school day Romeos or parental choices – this young lady remained single. It became clear that her fellow clerks, though charmed by her beauty, were somewhat intimidated by her competence and scared of her cloudy origins. These factors did not deter young Sarath Dissanayake who joined us for his first job as Staff Officer for Food Rations. Miss R was not a clerk in his Food Branch, but was called in one day to interpret the problems of a Tamil labourer. Sarath was bowled over at once. Nobody like her had ever swum into his ken either in his old school of Kosgolla Central or his circle of similarly inhibited rural boys in the Peradeniya campus.

With charming naivete, he confessed his infatuation to us, his older colleagues. He also admitted that he had never spoken to Miss R about this, apart from gazing longingly at her whenever she came in as an interpreter. We gently informed him of the long established hierarchy of the Kachcheri establishment where social relations with subordinate staff was just 'not done'. He reluctantly accepted our advice as to his conduct in office and, we all agreed, it was all above board. We failed to notice Miss R wearing any look of longing or triumph in having won the heart of a Staff Officer. And it soon became clear that it was a purely one-sided infatuation on Sarath's side. The poor chap became ever more despondent and badly felt the need to share his sorrows. One day he took the decisive step to write to Miss R and ask her hand in marriage. The very same day he left for Kosgolla to ask his parents' consent. He never came back.

A few days later, a simple village schoolmaster sought permission to interview the Government Agent and plead for his son Sarath who had, technically, 'vacated post'. The G.A. already knew the case. Miss Ratnayake had met him with Sarath's desperate letter and confessed it was a shock to her for she had never encouraged him, nor was she interested in marrying him. He then discussed it with us, his colleagues and confidants, and was prepared to handle Sarath's father. He assured the old gent that Miss R was no 'man-eater' and never wanted to marry his son. The G.A. would also arrange to have the lovesick youth transferred immediately to a distant outpost. All parties concerned, save poor Sarath, heaved sighs of relief.

Discovery

The case of poor Sarath and Miss R had long faded in my memory by the time the merry-go-round of transfers brought me to the same Kachcheri where I found an old friend and colleague from Aluth Eliya, Basnayake who had been Office Assistant. This was in Puranapura in the dry zone and my job was to resettle peasant farmers and inquire into land disputes. One day I invited Basnayake to join me on inspection to a very ancient Buddhist rock temple, now occupied by a few hermit monks whose title needed to be regularised. My friend was sorry he could not accompany me, but went on to say "You'll be passing the village of Puhulweva, where there is an unusual farmer you'd be interested to meet. This chap came to see me once about some permit or other. After some hemming and hawing he asked me whether, during my stint at Aluth Eliya Kachcheri I had met his daughter Imelda who had worked there. It took some time for it to click that farmer Ratnayake meant the Miss R who had driven poor Sarath crazy with love. I remembered her as an excellent officer, I assured him, and inquired after her. He said that she was now in some Ministry in Colombo. Our suspicions about her parentage were unfounded, after all. She does have a father. Meet the chap if you can spare the time."

A Japanese Garden

While I was passing Puhulweva village, on my way back from my discussions at the temple, I inquired about Ratnayake's farm to find that he was quite a local celebrity. I was given directions to "Japanwatte" as the farm was locally called. I was completely taken by surprise when I arrived to be warmly greeted by grizzled, but sturdy, Ratnayake. Instead of the ramshackle fences and haphazard cultivation typical of that region "Japanwatte" was an area as large as a playing field, sturdily fenced and methodically cultivated with a variety of vegetables. We got talking over many cups of ginger tea while his wife Thangamma, clearly Tamil in the drape of her saree, bustled about preparing our lunch. I asked my host why his land bore such a strange name, and heard an astounding story. "My second employer," said Ratnayaka, "was a Japanese gentleman Kawabata who worked in the then-famous paper merchants Nissei & Co. He was on the look-out for a reliable farm worker with a smattering of English, and had worked with foreigners. My earlier South American boss had given me an excellent recommendation which got me the job. We drove up to this land which was in jungle and hired almost all the men in Puhulweva to clear and level the land as flat as it could be. I settled down here with Thangamma, my wife, and strictly followed Mr.K's instructions as to what should be grown, and how. Our seeds were from Japan, and you can see how superbly they yet grow. No trees were ever to be grown, only vegetables.

"This was in the late '30s. War clouds loomed on the horizon and Japan was a possible enemy. But this meant nothing to us in quiet Puhulweva – till Mr. K's last hurried visit before he left for Japan. He then explained to me that this farm was to be an airstrip for Japanese planes that would arrive to liberate Ceylon from the British ! I was to follow his instructions to the letter, grow only vegetables and ensure that no branches overhung the area. A glorious future was to be mine when the Japanese won the war. I never saw him again.

"As you know the Japanese lost. But my own future had been assured. Thanks to Kawabata-san I am today the most prosperous farmer in Puhulweva."

Brumpy's Story

Over lunch I quietly asked Brumpy about his daughter Imelda of the Aluth Eliya convent. "She is not really my daughter, but Thangamma's. I married her before the baby was born and have treated her as my own and given her my name. It is a strange story. My first master was a South American, Mr. Race. He could never pronounce

Telephones:
1798 & 1799

Telegrams:
"NISEI"

P. O. Box
140

THE NISSEI TRADING CO.

FOR

: PAPER :

AND

STATIONERY

OF

Every Description

Proprietors of:—

The Ceylon Paper Box Manufacturing Company

Speciality:—

FOLDING PAPER BOXES FOR PACKING
:: CAKES, BUTTER, TEA, Etc. ::

AND

NISSEI FARM

(Rice and Vegetable Growers)
ANURADHAPURA.

Office & Stores:—

92-100, First Cross Street,
COLOMBO.

1938 advertisement for 'Japanwatte' vegetables

Ratnayaka' so he called me Brumpy. He lived down a sea-side lane in Wellawatta – where he led an exciting life. Writers and artists were in and out and had a wonderful time talking, carousing and listening to music all night long. He was a handsome young man, and many lovely ladies often slipped in, discreetly, to share his bed. But his love-life showed no snobbery. Thangamma was the buxom young 'coolie' who daily cleaned our toilets. Overwhelmed by passion one day he swept her off to his bed. And he never forgot her.

"The time came for Mr. Race to leave Ceylon. By which time Thangamma was clearly pregnant. My master had a proposition for me. He asked me to marry Thangamma to give her baby a father and his name. He would support mother and child as long as he lived. If the baby was a girl she should be named Imelda, after his own mother. He stood by his word and so did we. The baby girl born a few months after he left was named Imelda Ratnayake. The money was sent to us through Race's good friend, an artist in Kandy. It was he who suggested we send her to the Aluth Eliya convent for education and a genteel upbringing. Imelda never forgot us and even now, comes to Puhulweva to spend holidays with us. She now works in a Ministry in Colombo. Our great sadness is that she has not yet married. Her mother faults her for being too finicky and advises her not to wait for Prince Charming but settle for a quiet, decent boy. She just smiles. We are too old and she is too wise for us to guide her life ....."

It was an amazing story which raised more questions than it answered. I thanked Brumpy and went on my way – to share this information with Basnayaka and puzzle over the mysterious Mr. Race.

The Poet

Some years later the startling truth dawned on me when I read the Memoirs of the great Chilean poet, and Nobel laureate, Pablo Neruda. It was all there – his sojourn in Ceylon, his home in Wellawatta, Brumpy his retainer and .... the 'dusky statue' with whom he shared

Buxom young 'coolie'

'the lightning spasm of the flesh'. 'Pablo Neruda' was only his pen name. His real name was Ricardo Reyes – Brumpy's 'Mr. Race'! Meanwhile, the poet's daughter, Imelda, seemed to have disappeared without trace. I vaguely wondered whether she had ever discovered the identity of her famous father.

Some time after my retirement I found myself at an international conference of a professional association in Mexico City. It was a strange melange of luxury and poverty. Elegantly dressed women and men jostled along the pavements stepping over family groups of Maya Indians playing reed pipes for their ragged children to dance and beg a few pesos. Every hotel had such families clustered outside while armed guards patrolled the corridors and mariachi bands played in their ballrooms. It was in one such ballroom that we conferred.

A distinguished Chilean delegate walked up to me, introduced himself as Ronaldo Frei who had been an FAO expert in Sri Lanka. He invited me to dinner so that he could reminisce about our country. I gladly accepted to escape the boring official events laid on. As he walked up to greet me at the hotel lobby he was accompanied by his wife. She was a handsome woman with an intriguing smile, who seemed strangely familiar. As she stretched out her hand to shake mine she said "Sir, can't you recognize me? I am Imelda Ratnayake who worked in Aluth Eliya Kachcheri." It was a seismic shock for me.

As we dined, Ronaldo told me their story. He had always been enthralled by the poetry of Pablo Neruda and decided to come to Colombo so he could absorb the atmosphere his hero once strode in "heavy with splendours" in "pavilions of passional leafage ..... in the midst of a spindrift of verdure". He roamed the by lanes of Wellawatta armed with Neruda's Memoirs, and even pestered the old artist in Kandy, to find some clues as to the poet's life here. His persistence paid off and he located Brumpy and Thangamma in Puhulweva. This led him back to Imelda, whose olive Latin looks had first charmed him when he met her at an FAO meeting in Colombo. At last she had met her Prince Charming. And Ronaldo had won a living link with Pablo Neruda. And, as in all good fairy stories, they lived happily ever after.

HOW MUCH LAND .... ?

Coming from a family without an inch of land to call its own, it is an amusing irony that I was fated to spend most of my working life as a District Land Officer (DLO) distributing vast extents of government land to "deserving peasants" in every province of this country.

The strangely designated "Land Kachcheri" (L.K) central to the whole process of land distribution was an odd melange of bureaucracy, paternalism and (oddly enough) democracy. I faintly discerned its workings as a fledgling DLO in 1953 when I accompanied Trincomalee's Asst. Govt. Agent on his field trips. These events were usually held in an open-sided school hall – packed with villagers awaiting our arrival. The AGA took his seat at a large desk, flanked by the Divisional Revenue Officer (DRO) and the L.K. Clerk who unfolded a long foolscap sheet rather like an attendance register. The Village Headman (V.H.) stood by acting appropriately humble (to the AGA) and officious (to the villagers) as the need arose. I am afraid the proceedings made little sense to me as they were in Tamil – which I did not know. An announcement was first made before commencing operations. After that, as their names were called out humble villagers diffidently stepped forward one by one to face a brief cross examination duly recorded in the "L.K. Schedule" – a document inextricably woven into my official career for the next 25 years. We sat, without any break for lunch, till early evening when the last man or woman had been interviewed. Stilling the pangs of hunger on such occasions was the first lesson instilled into me by the AGA. "These poor men and women" he said "have come a long way to the LK and have nowhere to eat. They will resent our indifference to their plight if we take a lunch break while they stew in hunger. So let us also share their hunger and finish the job we came for !" A valuable lesson imparted by a caring man.Soon after this initial peep into the workings of a Kachcheri, the Land Commissioner decided that DLOs needed some knowledge of the rudiments of maps and surveying to do their job better. Three of us DLO were duly despatched to the survey school at Diyatalawa – for a brief training. We soon learnt that our gangs of labourers were far more adept than us in wielding tape measures, pickets and plane tables. We therefore exercised that invaluable tool of management – delegation. Once an appropriate fee had been negotiated we three swapped yarns in the eucalyptus shade while our gang surveyed slushy deniyas and winding footpaths with ease born of long practice. But we did learn to read and understand maps and survey plans and I acquired an undying fascination for the landscapes of maps and the intriguing place names they record.

Anuradhapura

Anuradhapura District is where I honed whatever "skills" I may have had as a DLO. My first Land Kachcheries were for Village Expansion (V.E.) schemes. Ancient "purana" villages were clustered cosily below their little village tanks and paddy fields. Disease, isolation and poverty had kept their populations stagnant and wants negligible. DDT had now banished malaria, better schools had eradicated illiteracy and access roads ended their isolation. The expanding population needed land and housing. V.E was the answer. Thanks (?) to the British most of the land around villages had been declared "Crown Land" at the disposal of the government. As there had been no conflicting interest from plantation crops in the Dry Zone a benevolently paternal policy had "mapped-out" each village neatly allocating specific areas for Village Forests (for firewood, fencing etc.), Pasture (for cattle), Community Purposes (School, playgrounds), andVillage Expansion (housing allotments). Whenever a need surfaced for more housing the VH and local officials made a rough census of the families who needed it. According to this identified need a Kachcheri Surveyor blocked out (on the plan) allotments on the land set apart for V.E. Community centred planning was undreamed of 45 years ago and, as a result, these new lots were unimaginatively strung along village roads instead of being clustered in cosy domesticity. Approaching any village on foot the VE lands ("badu idam") stick out like sore thumbs in dreary contrast to the homely huddle of the old village ("purana gama" / "sinnakkara idam").

Once the survey was done, an "LK Notice" was published in the village concerned. This announced that a certain number of blocks were available for "alienation" (i.e. distribution)to landless permanent residents. These would be allocated at an L.K. to be held on a specified date at a specified site. Written applications had to be made in advance. Once these applications were received they were listed in the "L.K. Schedule" which noted name, age, number of dependants, extent of land owned and period of residence in village.

Armed with this schedule and accompanied by a trusty clerk I drove off to the site of the LK to be met by the V.H and a crowd of village people – applicants, village worthies, and curious onlookers in an era devoid of other mass entertainment. Usually, the venue was the local school or Village Tribunal, occasionally the "bana maduwa" of the village temple. The village school was (yet is, I am afraid) a long half-walled building with a platform at one end from which the Headmaster surveyed all the classes clustered under one roof. Broken furniture cluttered one corner – awaiting condemnation by a Board of Survey. As soon as we occupied the head table and spread out our schedule there was a rush for the few available seats and it was amusing to see old folks and strapping adults scrunching themselves into the infants' chairs close to the platform. Children hung over the half-walls gaping at the curious goings-on. Decades ago, in Rajarata's more remote villages, little boys wore long shirts (diga kamisa) like cassocks, even to school. It was amusing to see them chasing each other hitching up their "skirts".

The VT courts were generally smaller than school halls and, deliberately, user – unfriendly. The judicial officer was ensconced on a high platform barricaded from the hoi-polloi compelled to remain standing humbly throughout the proceedings. These forbidding but ramshackle buildings were therefore used only when schools were in session and thus unavailable.

Land Kachcheri

The presiding DLO's table was flanked by a long bench to accommodate a "jury" of respected citizens who were expected to help evaluate the applicants. They were kingpins in a variety of local organizations – Village Councils, Rural Development Societies, Dayaka Sabhas, Death Donation Associations etc. Each applicant who stepped forward, when his name was called out, had to answer a litany of questions. Age? Length of residence in village? Married? How many children? Their ages? Occupation? Extent of land owned? Special claims? In a little village, where everybody knew each other, the responses were largely truthful. It was not easy to make false claims before the jury of advisers and the whole assembled village. Newcomers were automatically disqualified. The desired qualifications were permanent residence, landlessness and a large family. Odd little facts emerged during questioning. One man who claimed to have fathered an extraordinary number of children was closely questioned by me as their ages seemed to overlap. The assembly guffawed when he shyly confessed to living in amicable polygamy with two sisters.

In retrospect, the LK was an exercise in participatory democracy. It was up to the DLO to win the crowd over by convincing them of his objectivity and independence of any partiality which may be displayed by the V.H. Bawling at applicants or officious attitudes and jargon had to be avoided at all cost. Audience rapport had to be established. The best way was a readiness to entertain comments from the audience which often produced valuable insights into village needs or a salty comment on a dubious applicant.

Selections were not announced at the LK – although they had broadly been decided on at this public conclave. Back at the Kachcheri the list of selectees was perused, checked and finalized. It was then sent for public display in the village and written objections, if any, were invited. Once these were received the DLO held another open inquiry, aided by his "jury", to decide on the validity of any objections which would disqualify a proposed selectee. The final list was then published. All that remained was for the Surveyor to point out the boundaries and hand them over to the selectees. They were now transformed into "allottees", proud holders of a permit under the Land Development Ordinance and entitled to a variety of subsidies from a generous government – for houses, wells, latrines etc. – pursuing an old British Governor's utopian dream of a "sturdy self-reliant peasantry"!

Galle

The whirligig of Govt Service transferred me away from the simple peasant communities of Rajarata, where there was ample land for the landless, to the complex social groupings of Southern Ruhuna where demand for land far exceeded supply. I was warned that I would be walking on eggshells holding LK's in this cradle of hot-bloods. My first LK was to allocate minute allotments for housing fishermen in a coastal area. Taking my warning to heart I was painfully euphemistic when I questioned the first few applicants as to whether they were "engaged in the fisheries industry " (dheevara karmantha). These grizzled old salts could not make much sense of this absurd query. "No – Sir ! I am a fisherman (malu karaya)!" I stood corrected and, greatly relieved, carried on the L.K. with its usual mix of honest questioning and good humoured blarney.

Competition for land was very heavy in Galle district as there was hardly any "Crown land" available for "alienation" (phrases integral to land policy). Strips of land, grudgingly extracted from estates, were converted into housing lots. There was no question of land for subsistence farming – it was for homes for wage-earning people who could not be described as "peasants". The LK schedule had to become more refined in its classification. Was the man employed in this division ? Did his wife and family live here ? Was his income too high to qualify for free (almost) Crown land ? Hidden animosities surfaced at objection time and adjudicating claims was quite a headache. However, the tried old formula of consultation with local officials and "jury" invariably produced an acceptable list of selectees.

Youth Settlers

The colonization schemes under the great reservoirs of the Dry Zone had been planned to absorb a quota of landless persons from the land-hungry South. Each district was given its quota. But it was no easy job to whip up enthusiasm among southerners to leave their lush green homeland to pioneer under the blazing sun of the Dry Zone – far from their kith and kin. But the few bold spirits who ventured out did make good.

In the late fifties Youth Settlements were planned as a solution to unemployment. "Take these young rascals out of their villages" said the Minister "and make them Dry Zone farmers". Youth LK's were held with this end in view. I used all my powers of persuasion, and my familiarity with the Dry Zone, to make these sceptical young chaps agree to become colonists. The response was far from overwhelming – but a bold few did volunteer.

Back in Anuradhapura, once again, I had the unusual experience of welcoming to Padaviya Scheme the same youths I had earlier selected from Galle. They were happy to meet a familiar face, a tenuous link with their southern home. I stood in "loco parentis" to them, settling them initially in dormitories, allocating sympathetic overseers who saw to their needs, and ensuring their timely subsidy payments. Little by little they fulfilled their promise, built homes, married and many embarked on business with customary Southern ingenuity.

Twenty odd years later, while serving in Trincomalee, I visited this now bustling settlement of "former youths". They had named it Tissapura. "After which King? Devanampiya Tissa or Saddha Tissa ?" I asked them. "No" they replied – "it was after the young DLO who led us to this land of promise!". It would have been flattery had they guessed the identity of the inquisitive stranger. But they did not. And a once-young-DLO left the scene with his head in the clouds.

Mutual Trust

This account of the now-lost ritual of a land kachcheri carries no reference to MP's because in that era they were never ubiquitous. There existed a civic consensus and mutual trust between politicians and district officials. Our integrity and judgement were taken for granted. Never did any MP attempt to impose a pre-selected list at an LK. He relied on the sound opinions of his voters expressed in the participatory democracy of the LK process. And this system worked.

After twenty-five years distributing hundreds (may be thousands) of acres of "Crown land" to "deserving peasants" I bade a fond farewell to all Kachcheries – ruefully conscious that I yet remained as landless as when I hesitantly stepped into my first, and coincidentally last, Kachcheri in Trincomalee.

NUWARA ELIYA
"ALUTH ELIYA"

A BLUE *"MANAME"* AT GOODWOOD

1957 was a heady year for me. I had just been transferred to the Kachcheri at Nuwara Eliya as District Land Officer. No longer was I under the avuncular eye of a more senior colleague, as I had earlier been in Trincomalee, Galle and Anuradhapura. It was both exciting and rather intimidating to feel that the fate and fortunes of many thousand peasants on 'Crown' land lay now in my, rather inexperienced, hands. My chief, Manders the Government Agent, was the last British Civil Servant in the country. He had chosen this little district to wind up his career, among its mists and soughing pines, hobnobbing with his fellow countrymen yet lording it over the 'thottam' or carousing in their Planters' Clubs. He ran our Kachcheri with a very loose rein and left his young D.L.O to his own devices. Thrown in at the deep end, I had no alternative but to swim.

Not long after I arrived in N'Eliya I fell in with a group of kindred spirits who had been my University contemporaries and were now in charge of various government departments here – Archives, Agriculture, Electricity and Food Control. It didn't take us long to move out of our respective guesthouses and into our own home at 'Shanti Alaya' on a steep hillock, not far from the brewery. We were soon joined by the CCS Cadet who was assigned to the Kachcheri to learn his 'land work' from me. He was fresh out of the University at Peradeniya and a loyal acolyte of Sarachchandra whose epoch making 'Maname' had stormed Sinhala drama a few months earlier. His spirited rendering of its wonderful lyrics proved a counterpoint to the Engineer's full-throated versions of Rupasinghe Master's 'golden oldies' as we drummed our accompaniment on the dining table.

Poramadulla

Nuwara Eliya district was not all tea estates, pines and misty mountain tops. Its lower reaches sloped right down to the Mahaweli at Walapane. In another direction it included the administrative division of Uda Hewaheta whose boundary was a scant twelve miles from Kandy. This was a bonanza for the bachelors of Shanti Alaya who spent our weekends with bonhomous friends in Colombo and drowsily drove up on Monday mornings to our distant duty station. We had evolved a model exercise in time and motion study to suit our needs. En route from Colombo we briefly detoured to the Peradeniya Campus where our friend, the Cadet, bade a reluctant farewell to his beloved. Our next stop was at Teldeniya where another colleague awaited us with his 'taxi fare' - a bulging 'buth mula' of red rice and 'ambulas' in Kandyan style prepared by his doting mother.

The D.R.O's office at Hanguranketa gave us a chance to stretch our legs and go through the 'land files' of the villages we were due to visit. As we drove past Rikillagaskada and Poramadulla I was flooded with fond memories of childhood days. Way back in 1942 when Ceylon quaked at the prospect of a Japanese invasion, our friends the Wimalasenas of Ekiriya welcomed us 'evacuees' into their family home, to live there till the war was over. It was an idyllic holiday where we town dwelling children immersed ourselves joyfully in the rhythms of a Kandyan village. Alas! The Japanese invasion never came. Our idyll ended, and we crept back reluctantly to our street-fronting home and forgotten school books.

In that age and time MPs were not yet so omnipresent or omnipotent, as to overshadow even Kachcheri officers as young as we were. It was for this reason that, after inspecting land for the school playing field, the Principal of Poramadulla Central College invited us to be guests of honour at a sitting of the school's Model Parliament. The Cabinet of that era was small enough to be comfortably seated on the school stage. The 'Minister of Health' was a charming young thing in the 'lama sari' and 'lovichchiya', the preferred school uniform during that brief flowering of nationalist fervour. The 'MPs' were an articulate lot and raised many relevant questions which the 'Ministers' answered as best as they could. It was a lively exchange and showed us how alive to national issues were these young people – these 'children of Kannangara'. What brought the House down was when a cheeky 'MP' asked the lady 'Minister' – "Madam Minister, what is the truth about your relationship with X (a religious dignitary)?" (This was a notorious scandal at the time). Without batting an eyelid the 'Minister' retorted "My private life is my own and cannot be the subject of Parliamentary debate. Please restrict your questions to the Ministry of Health". Laughter and applause greeted this put down. I wonder what the future held for this quick-witted lass, by now a matron in her fifties.

Stiff Climbs and Water Spouts

Climbing the hills of Uda Hewaheta was both exhausting and exhilarating. The pungent scent of 'mana' grass, the scratchy shrubs of the intrusive lantana, resting on a wayside log to catch our breath and tapping the postman for local gossip remain an unforgettable experience – now wafted beyond recall by the winds of time. The purpose of our inspections was to inspect peasant cottages built on government allotments and approve subsidy payments or to hold 'land kachcheries' to distribute land holdings to homeless villagers clustered hopefully in little open sided schoolrooms.

After the job was done, it was time to reward ourselves. We had already mapped out the most likely spots for our picnic lunch. It had to be by a gushing 'peella' or waterspout where a brook tumbled down from wooded hillsides. A favoured spot was at Mooloya – once the site of a Police shooting which is etched in the history of militant trade unionism. Such matters did not concern us as we stripped down to basics and shudderingly surrendered our sweaty bodies to the bracing cold of the water spout. And after that, the glorious home-cooked repast from Teldeniya, eaten off banana leaves. On our way back to N'Eliya via Padiyapelella we cast more than a passing glance at the bathing maids at the Kumbal-gamuva waterspout – which we had, half-jestingly, been warned to avoid. Local legend had it that any youth who bathed there fell willing victim to one of these lovely sirens and never went back home!

These were the days when an important element of land policy in the Kandyan areas was 'strip acquisition for village expansion'. This was an attempt to recompense peasants for the takeover of their ancestral lands for British plantations by means of the pernicious Waste Lands Ordinance. Age old villages were now rural slums, cottages clustered together, hemmed in by a sea of tea. Our job was to acquire land from the surrounding plantations so that the expanding population of the villages could be settled in a planned manner. The Acquisition Inquiries we held were reminiscent of a dental surgery – so painful to the Superintendent was the extraction of even a little strip of 'his' estate land. Our reward was the gratitude of the new allottees, who often disproved the gloomy forecasts of the former owners by tending with loving care the tea which was now their very own.

'Goodwood' near Poramadulla was one such acquired estate, probably named after the famous racecourse by a Briton of yore with a passion for the 'sport of gentlemen'. During my tenure in N'Eliya it became a pleasant settlement of sturdily built cottages nestling in a mosaic of vegetable gardens and lush tea. The 'allottees', the quaint official term for these settlers, were all from the villages around and were an integral part of the community in all its social and religious activities.

A Blue 'Maname'

Many villages of Uda Hewaheta yet preserved a centuries old tradition of folk drama, enacted during the Sinhala New Year season. I retained a vivid memory of that vigorous folk epic 'Sokari' being performed from dusk to dawn on the Wimalasena's lawn, way back in the year of the Japanese invasion that never took place. The vigorous dancing, the youths in women's costume, the salty humour, the throb of drums and the flaring acetylene lamps made an indelible impression on my boyhood imagination. It was wonderful that the tradition yet remained and I was determined to experience it again.

I was too young an officer to be entitled to a 'command performance'. I therefore requested the Village Headman, an indispensable fount of local knowledge, to see whether he could arrange for us to be in the audience when one of the old folk dramas was next being performed. An all night Sokari was not feasible just yet, but one such drama was being played next week in Goodwood. We arranged our field visit so that we could take in the performance and later spend the night in a nearby Circuit Bungalow. You can imagine the thrill we had when we were told that it was the 'Maname Nadagama' to be performed – the true folk drarma from whose rough clay Sarachchandra had fashioned his timeless masterpiece.

The whole village was there, squatting on the compound in front of the village Community Centre. We were, to our embarrassment, honoured with the only two chairs with a gaggle of irreverent and curious children clustering at our feet. The "stage" was the hard earth of the volleyball court and lit by flaring acetylene lamps. The play began with the cavortings of clownish 'bahubothayas' who had the children in fits of laughter. Then came the Gurunnanse who introduced this Jataka tale in a rather reedy voice. Prince Maname then strode in performing his ritualised sword play to the dramatic throb of drums. I remember but few of the details of the performance as such. The most dramatic entrance, as in Sarachchandra's, was that of the Veddha King. Whereas Sarachchandra's Veddha was a true wild man, rangy and athletic in his skimpy skirt, the 'Goodwood Veddha' was a dark, sombre and majestic presence. His entrance was a magnificent bit of stagecraft that I can never forget. He was a broadly built man dressed in regal splendour and gifted with a magnificent mop of hair, like a now popular god-man. He strode in tossing his glorious hair and releasing huge puffs of blue dust into the air, every time he shook his royal head. Liberal handfuls of washing blue had been worked into his hair to achieve this effect which earned the 'oohs' and "aahs" of the spectators. The young man who acted the Princess could, of course, never achieve the tantalising hip wiggle of the University Princess. But he danced with vim and vigour the role of the faithless jade to her well-deserved end.

It must, however, be understood that this 'original' was completely different in interpretation from the moral ambiguity so integral to Sarachchandra's version. This was a true morality play in stark black and white and thus close to the original Jataka with no sympathy wasted on the faithless Princess. And the Nadagama made this point abundantly clear when she falls down, abandoned and dead, while a passing jackal sniffs round the body and then cocks his hind leg over it to bestow the last insult – to the vast amusement of the groundlings.

Almost fifty years have passed since this Maname graced the hard earth of Goodwood, its actors have long since departed, grown old are my boon companions of yore and 1957, that magical year of our golden youth, is fast receding into the mists of time.

THE DANCER ON THE HILL

"No, young lady" said the D.R.O. with a fatherly smile 'I just cannot recommend you for a block of land so long as you are unmarried. Come back when you have found yourself a husband and let's see what we can do". I heard the tail end of this conversation as I walked into the office of the Divisional Revenue Officer (D.R.O) at Hanguranketa, the main town of Uda Hewaheta. I had come down from Nuwara Eliya Kachcheri on my field visit to look into 'land matters'. He was speaking to a sturdy young woman dressed neatly in Kandyan saree who had come to plead her case one Division Day. She was clearly reluctant to take 'no' for an answer and, not overawed by us officials, firmly repeated "I do not want a land to build a house, but to put up a school for dancing!" Amused at this unusual request the D.R.O restated the standard formula "Government lands are allocated only for residential purposes or cultivation – and never to unmarried persons. Ask the D.L.O. who is now with me if that isn't the case." She now addressed me with polite exasperation. "Sir, I am a fully trained Kandyan dancer and my guru is Sri Jayana. Rather than teach in a government school and drum away for reluctant schoolgirls I am determined to establish a dancing school of my own and teach Kandyan dancing to village boys and girls who are really interested." I was intrigued by this bold and most unusual request – but also aware of the strait-jacket of regulations and precedent. So I sought refuge in the standard ploy of government service – postponement. "All right, one of these days we will inspect the land you have asked for before we make any decision".

Lunch at any D.R.O's home was always memorable – especially to bachelor staff officers accustomed to the stodgy, uninspired food of chummery cooks. The cuisine of the Uda Hewaheta D.R.O's home was doubly memorable as his wife was a superb cook. Over a scrumptious lunch when we rehashed the day's events and the case of Ransina (that was the dancer's name) our hostess chided us for being cynical and conservative in our attitude. We should encourage this brave young woman in her chosen metier instead of pushing her into dull matrimonial dependence. She was sure that regulations could always be bent and our moral duty was to find a way to help this pioneer who deserved all praise. Shamefacedly we undertook to do what we could.

Back at the Kachcheri other concerns occupied my time and the case of the articulate dancer seemed of little urgency. Two, or rather three, things shook me into making good my undertaking to inspect the land she was applying for. The first was an official reminder from the D.R.O. The second was my responsibility to train the young C.C.S. cadet newly assigned to me to acquire experience in 'land work'. The third was the Cultural Revolution of 1956 that had just burst upon us and had an enthusiastic exponent in our Cadet, an acolyte of the legendary Sarathchandra. I could postpone matters no longer.

The Field Inspection

After due notice to the D.R.O. (to ensure ourselves an excellent lunch) we set off down the High Forest-Maturata-Padiyapelella road whose many hairpin bends, tremendous precipices and rugged surface were a truly mind blowing experience. The bold and rash drivers that we were, we relished the adrenalin surge of swinging round a bend with tires slipping on the slippery grass, inches from a perpendicular fall or scraping by a rickety lorry in an inadequate lay-by. Ah! carefree youth !

We picked up the D.R.O. at Hanguranketa and drove along to the land that Ransina was applying for. The Village Headman (V.H.) awaited us together with Ransina, her parents and the usual knot of curious fellow villagers who straggled along behind our inspection team. The path led through a pleasant little village with straw thatched huts, a patch of paddy-fields, an ancient 'ambalama' and a few 'LDO houses' built with dull uniformity. The latter indicated we had now left the 'purana' village and were on 'Crown Land' (the quaint Colonial term then in use). A short climb up a barren slope devoid of any trees and covered with rough 'mana' grass brought us to the summit of a little hillock. We looked around for the site proposed for the school and saw no likely place, by conventional criteria. Ransina surprised us all by saying that the summit of the hill was exactly what she needed. It was sufficiently distant from the other houses for the drumming not to be a nuisance. But it was accessible for the village children whom she proposed to teach. The fact that this hillock was devoid of vegetation and water meant that it had held no attraction to landless encroachers (the bane of D.L.Os). It was obvious that the V.H's report (usually taken with a hefty pinch of salt) was quite accurate in this case – that there were no 'competing claims' for this windswept hillock. The land was free for allocation. But Ransina's eligibility for selection and her capacity to set up this school had yet to be established. Her parents stood guarantee and shrewd questioning by the veteran D.R.O satisfied us that her elders and peers down in the village would support her bold venture. Instant decisions are never the practice when it comes to allocating land. So a rather disappointed Ransina had to be content with our parting assurance that we would communicate our decision in due course.

Where there is a will .....

Back at the D.R.O's bungalow we sat down to (in today's jargon) a 'power lunch' where we discussed the case of this pioneer "women's libber" so tellingly advocated by our hostess. It was clearly not possible to allocate her a 'housing allotment' – neither did she want this. One possibility, involving a lengthy process and much correspondence with the Land Commissioner in Colombo, was granting a Long Term Lease to a properly constituted corporate body for a clearly defined purpose. The D.R.O. was fairly sure he could convince a group of village worthies, with Ransina as its executive, to form such a body as they were already backing her venture. But this would take time, and it was doubtful how long their enthusiasm would last while the slowly meandering flow of government correspondence wound to a finish. I had a flash of inspiration – an Annual Permit. This was a most impermanent form of land holding generally given to stall holders on road reservations on condition that they would have to quit whenever the 'Crown' required the land. We were confident that the 'Crown' would never have any conceivable use for this barren, waterless hillock and that an Annual Permit would be the quickest way of handing over the land to Ransina – if she would be satisfied with this impermanent tenure. Backed by his wife, the D.R.O. undertook to explain matters to the dancer. The Cadet and I left for Nuwara Eliya happy that we had, hopefully, done our little bit for traditional culture.

All's well

Everything went well. Ransina agreed to our formula. I signed the Annual Permit and posted it to the D.R.O. who then formally handed it over and allocated the land to her. Months passed. One fine day we received a gratefully phrased invitation to the inauguration of Ransina's Kalayatanaya. This was an era when political VIPs were not particularly sought after for village functions. Thus it was that the D.R.O, Cadet and I had the honour of being escorted up the hill by a bevy of little dancing girls and a drummer. An impressive cadjan structure now adorned the hill-top with a hall for dancing and a level compound in front. Ransina's supporters had clearly rallied round. We were traditionally greeted with sheaves of betel by Ransina herself gloriously colourful in Kandyan dancer's costume, and seated in places of honour. However, the chief guest, appropriately, was her guru Sri Jayana to whom she paid deep obeisance before commencing her dance recital. There was a welcome minimum of speeches and her gratitude was shown in the dancing of her little pupils and the magnificent vigour of her own dance.

It was deeply satisfying that we had constructively bent the rules

Led by dancing girls

to help a truly talented artiste and an extraordinarily determined young woman to achieve her unusual (for that time) ambition to establish her own rural centre to foster traditional Kandyan dance. The tortuous process of issuing a Long Term Lease had not yet been finalised when I left Nuwara Eliya on transfer a few years later – by which time it was reported that the Kalayatanaya was firmly on its feet.

Musing over the years gone by, I wonder whether the hills and fields of her little village yet echo to the throbbing of drums and the jingle of anklets from Ransina's school.

RED CARDIGAN, YELLOW BOOTS

When the merry-go-round of government transfers moved me to Aluth Eliya from Puranapura I found myself not only in another kachcheri town but in another world. My last night in the ancient town was spent as a lodger in a decrepit old walauwa surrounded by an expanse of paddy fields, falling asleep to the eerie howling of jackals hunting. My first night in Aluth Eliya was spent in a mock English manor house set in a flourishing garden of poppies, hollyhocks, roses, lilies and other 'European' flowers whose names I knew not. No longer did a mosquito net protect my sleeping self from whining insects. I was in an incredibly Englishy bedroom with flowery cretonne curtains, ensconced in a cocoon of soft blankets and sheets neatly tucked in all round. I had dined, rather diffidently, off unaccustomed cutlery and with great relish a rather Dickensian dinner of soup, steak and veg rounded off with pudding and custard ! I was now a resident (temporary) of a guest house glorying in the name of Waterston Manor located on Buttercup Drive – a rather up-market sounding address I flaunted to friends and family while I could.

My hostess was Mrs. Bertie Perera, a dark, motherly lady who presided over the occupants of Waterston. Apart from me, these were mainly honeymooners and families on holiday escaping from the hot humidity of the low country to inhale the piney breezes and shiver deliciously in the cold mist as they enthusiastically trudged the flower-filled parks and wooded paths of Aluth Eliya. When I had time to settle down and look around I became intrigued by the Perera family. Bertie Perera was a handsome man, obviously much younger than his wife who doted on him. He dressed with almost foppish elegance that I envied – herringbone tweed sports coat, discreetly checked Viyella shirt, Tootal tie, Daks slacks and Dolcis brogues. This is what he wore to work as the Chief Clerk in the dusty old office of the Roads Engineer ! When dusk fell he wore a natty blazer, and a silk Ascot replaced his tie. His car was a cherry red Triumph roadster with a sporty roar that he drove in flashy style. There was also one other person whom I saw every morning, a lovely tall teen-age schoolgirl who set off wearing a red cardigan (de rigeur for local convent girls trooping along to school like a gaggle of giggling red penguins) hugging a pile of books. What made her distinct from the rest of her peers were the primrose yellow wellington boots she wore unlike the dull black boots all others wore to protect themselves from the slushy paths. She was Mrs. Perera's sister though she seemed over twenty years younger. Once in a rare while their mother was glimpsed, a wizened bent old lady puttering around in the kitchen garden adjoining her little room.

Peace Haven

I found myself in the unaccustomed luxury of Waterston Manor as I knew nobody in Aluth Eliya, and an affluent uncle, unaware of my limited means, recommended it to me as he had spent holidays there. Soon after I settled down to work in the quaint wooden Kachcheri I discovered that I did know a few staff officers who had been at the University, down Thurstan Road, around my time. The Archivist, the Engineer and the Food Controller shared a 'chummery' which they invited me to join. I lost no time in checking out 'Peace Haven' and found it most congenial – an untidy bachelor home reminiscent of undergrad rooms, complete with comic cook. I lost little time in moving my bags from Waterston to Peace Haven – though with some regret at losing its cosy bedroom and superb cuisine. The raucous camaraderie of my new household was more attuned to my temperament. I seemed to detect some slight regret in Mrs. Perera's expression when I bade her good-bye but I put it down to my imagination as she would have been quite accustomed to birds of passage flitting through Waterston.

The Engineer, Peace Haven's Oldest Resident, was the Head of the Department whose Chief Clerk was Bertie Perera. It did not take me long to discover how this dapper young man came to marry his distinctly older wife. It was a classic tale that was reenacted many times over in outstation towns where widow ladies took in bachelor staff officers as lodgers. Mrs. Thomas had the best run hostelry in Aluth Eliya – though much more modest than Waterston. When a younger Bertie arrived on transfer, he settled down there for a short while – or so he thought. He had never imagined the quality of the tender loving care that Mrs. Thomas' dark and buxom daughter lavished on him ! Bertie became so comfortably ensconced that he never left the Thomas household. Less than a year later, wedding bells rang for Bertie Perera and Philomena Thomas. The new Mrs. Bertie was blessed with vision, and Bertie had shrewd financial savvy. Old Mrs. Thomas took a back seat while the Pereras moved into the cobwebby old place that was Waterston and transformed it into the up market guest house it now was. Mrs. Bertie's little sister, who had been a toddler when Bertie first moved into the Thomas household, had now blossomed into Petunia, the lissome schoolgirl in yellow wellingtons I had seen every morning at Waterston.

As I settled down to the routine of field inspections, gruelling climbs to hilltop settlements and Village Council elections rounded off with evenings of bar and billiards at the Public Services Club, Waterston Manor faded away from my consciousness. Once in a rare while I saw Petunia riding back home with Bertie in his red sports car. I had no reason to revisit Waterston being fully engaged in the rambustious life at Peace Haven and regular weekend forays to Colombo to court my fiancee with flowers and apples from the hills. Several months rolled by, and our Engineer with a roving eye for the lovelier girls in town, reported that the fair Petunia had left school and had begun work as a secretary in an insurance company. She could be seen briskly walking to work, dressed far more nattily than in school uniform, and clearly recognizable by her bright yellow wellingtons. Off and on, at closing time, Bertie's red sportster could be seen outside the insurance office to take Petunia home. Mrs. Perera was hardly ever seen in the car. She trudged to market every morning, lumpily wrapped up against the cold, accompanied by a wizened old 'boy' to carry back the provisions she had bought.

Donald Arrives

One evening at the club I was pleasantly surprised to meet Donald, an old school mate with whom I had lost touch ever since I went to University and he went – I knew not where. He had been an outstanding cricketer and captained our First XI. His good looks easily won him numerous schoolgirl fans who voted enthusiastically to award him the Most Popular School Cricketer of the Year. His sporting prowess easily gained him a place in the Police. He had now been promoted Inspector and transferred to Aluth Eliya range to take over as Officer-in-Charge of Dikgala a few miles out of town. Meanwhile, he told us he was at Waterston Manor till his predecessor vacated his official bungalow at Dikgala. The hospitable bachelors of Peace Haven invited him to join our jolly band. Rather reluctantly he declined the offer on the excuse that his stay there would only be for a few weeks. We believed his explanation and, when his bungalow fell vacant, helped him to instal his spartan household goods and throw a boozy house-warming party.

We began to hear that Bertie Perera's car was seen occasionally with an 'L' board and were faintly amused at the prospect of his rather large wife squeezing herself behind the steering wheel. But when we saw the car one Sunday being driven in typical jerky 'L' board style – it was Petunia at the wheel with Bertie gently coaching her – apparently as a brotherly gesture !

It soon became clear that our friend Donald had fallen headlong in love with Petunia at first sight whom he saw tripping along the flowery paths of Waterston in her trademark yellow boots. As soon as he found out that none of the bachelors of Peace Haven were in the running, he confessed his infatuation to us and we, in turn, promised him our fullest support. Of an evening we saw his battered Ford at the insurance company to give Petunia a lift home. We heard from him that whenever he dropped Petunia home Mrs. Bertie would invite him in and lay out a sumptuous tea. His courtship seemed to be going fine. The young couple was seen at the movies and even dancing at the Public Services Club, smilingly chaperoned by an approving Mrs. Bertie. These days Bertie himself was hardly ever seen at the Club which he had frequented almost daily. Our Engineer also reported that he wore a hang-dog expression at work and wasn't his usual cheery self.

Donald's courtship was firmly discouraged by his parents who had a line up of dowried maidens ready for inspection by their eligible son. A guest house keeper's sister was absolutely unthinkable. Donald had to move fast to forestall his family's likely plots. Time was of the essence and he enlisted the Peace Haven team to assist him. Petunia was ready and willing and, fortunately, over eighteen. The Kachcheri Registrar was contacted under oath of secrecy, a Special Licence was obtained and the shortest possible Notice of Marriage was given – but never exhibited. One fine morning Petunia set off for work as usual. A short while later Donald called over at her office escorted by the Peace Haven team in a back-up vehicle for any contingency. Her understanding boss gave Petunia leave of absence pronto. Our mini-convoy whisked the young couple to the Registry a short distance away. The Registrar, my colleague, was on stand by and in double quick time their marriage was registered with the Engineer and me as witnesses. The happy couple whizzed off to their honeymoon on the eastern coast, pre-empting any possible parental plots and stratagems.

Wedded Bliss

Donald and Petunia were very happy and the once bare Police bungalow was transformed into a lovely cottage, tastefully furnished and curtained. Its vases were full of flowers brought regularly by Mrs. Bertie who had, after a mild show of disapproval, forgiven her sister's impetuous marriage. She showered the young couple with an almost suffocating affection and visited them as often as she could, laden with flowers, fruit and food. Bertie accompanied her wearing a bored expression which we bachelors of Peace Haven attributed to his missing his evenings at the club. But this pattern gradually began to change. Donald's duties took him often to faraway tea estates or inaccessible villages to investigate knifings, murders or suicides. Petunia was left companionless in the cold and gloomy evenings when the monsoon wind rattled the 'takarang' roof. On my way back from field visits I had to pass by Donald's bungalow and found Bertie's red car often parked in the porch. I dropped in myself hoping to share some of the scrumptuous food that Mrs. Bertie always brought along but, to my disappointment, found Bertie there by himself carrying on a lively conversation with Petunia. He had clearly got over his initial reluctance to call on the young couple. Being curious by nature, Peace Haven residents compared notes and observed that Bertie's visits almost always coincided with Donald's trips on duty away from Dikgala. We knew that Petunia was very lonely. Their bungalow stood on a wind-swept hillock and her only neighbours were the wives of constables in their dingy barracks who kept a wary distance from their boss's wife. Donald's parents had disowned him and we were his only friends in the town. Social graces were not our forte, so our visits to their bungalow were restricted to an occasional dinner. We did not, however, miss Donald's company as he began meeting us once again at the Club with surprising frequency. Petunia was hardly ever with him and we presumed she was visiting her sister at Waterston for cosy chats. But Donald wasn't his usual cheery self and sat glumly at the bar, drinking rather heavily most days.

High Drama

A month or so before their first wedding anniversary a drama unfolded with a tragic speed that shattered many lives and left Aluth Eliya reeling with shock. Donald was on his way back to Dikgala one stormy evening, after an inquiry into a bloody brawl in a line-room in a faraway estate, when he was flagged down by a policeman on a motor-bike who had been despatched with an urgent message. A car had crashed down a precipice at a lonely hairpin bend somewhere between Dikgala and Aluth Eliya. A passing motorist had seen the swerving tyre marks, the wreck of a car far below with its headlights pointing skyward and heard faint cries. He rushed to the nearest Police Station, Dikgala.

The Sergeant in charge mounted a rescue party and sent a despatch rider to contact Donald. He arrived on a scene lit only by the dim torches of policemen and estate workers scrambling down the steep and muddy slope towards the wreckage. With characteristic generalship he sent for an ambulance and climbed down the fateful slope. I can only imagine his turmoil when he saw that the wreck was Bertie's red car, smashed beyond redemption, with a 'L' board on the buffer, fluttering damply in the biting wind. His Sergeant, who accompanied him, later told us of the icy efficiency he brought to the shocking spectacle of Petunia trapped behind the steering wheel, unconscious and moaning in pain. Bertie's broken body was by her side, clearly beyond resuscitation. He gently extricated her from the shambles, carrying her in his arms for the last time in his life. Petunia and Bertie were carried up the muddy slope in improvised stretchers to the waiting ambulance in which they rode together for the very last time – to hospital. Donald drove up in his jeep straight to Peace Haven where we were entrusted the responsibility of taking Mrs. Bertie to hospital to confront her double tragedy.

Last Chapter

We never saw Donald again. He drove back to Dikgala Police Station and, with customary thoroughness, wrote up an objective account of the accident in the Information Book. The rest is conjecture, as there were no witnesses. He went back to their bungalow, lay down on their bed with their wedding picture by his side – and shot himself in the head with his service revolver.

There is little more to be said. We were his only 'family' at Donald's funeral in Aluth Eliya's sombre, cypress shadowed graveyard. This town held bitter memories for me and I left soon after on transfer to a town by the sea. Months later my friends in Peace Haven told me that the doctor who had attended to Petunia, a young man named Coleridge, had proposed to her and been accepted. Soon after they married and emigrated to Australia. Mrs. Bertie gave up Waterston and led a sad life as a lodger in some distant cousin's home. A few years later I read her obituary – and her whole sad story was revealed in the notice:

> "The death is announced of Mrs. Philomena Perera
> (formerly of Waterston Manor, Aluth Eliya)
> widow of the late Bertie Perera and
> ***mother*** of Petunia (Mrs. Coleridge)".

THE CURIOUS EXPLOSION

One of those ephemeral pop stars of the 1960s had a song that went (to the best of my failing memory)

"Those were the days, my friend
We thought that they would never end .....
We had joy, we had fun
We had seasons in the sun ...."

that seems to sum up the carefree life of our bachelor home (we scorned the term chummery) 'Himalaya' in the 50s-up amidst the pines and mists of Aluth Eliya. We were all government 'staff officers' handling a variety of responsibilities in that district capital. Between us we dispensed electricity, supervised farms, controlled food rations, distributed land and even cared for old books. By fortunate coincidence we were from the same cohort of the University (then, the one and only) at Thurstan Road and had much in common. Official responsibility was balanced by happy irresponsibility and high fun off hours, swanking around town or whizzing about in new cars hoping to impress, with varying degrees of success, the all-too-few local lovelies or the sophisticated young socialites who invaded our town during the Season to saucily saunter the flower-bright parks or enjoy a mild flutter at the Racecourse. Those lucky enough embarked on brief, bitter-sweet encounters to emerge heart-whole to while away evenings and tickle others' envy with tales of assignations amidst pinewoods or overgrown churchyard. The cinema was another refuge. Rushing back to 'Himalaya' after a day of climbing distant hills on inspection we rang the obliging manager up to hold back the film till we turned up. Meanwhile a bemused audience was subjected to an overlong intermission. Big fish were we, in the little pond of Aluth Eliya!

A Colourful Bouquet

In that era, a mere decade or so after Independence, Aluth Eliya yet basked in the cosy complacency of a colonial hill station. The last British Civil Servant was our Government Agent reliving youthful memories of pines, mists, mock – Tudor cottages and planters' clubs (yet largely "white"). Planters' memsahibs drove into town to stock up to provisions at old English firms or tried and tested local shops staffed by obsequious salesmen. And the town was home to a colourful bouquet of characters who entertained us no end. There was the tipsy old reporter who was a fount of ribald limericks; the planter abandoned by his wife who mournfully trotted his enormous St. Bernard round Lake Gregory every evening; the decrepit Englishman who earned his tipple by hiring out his services and his huge old Chevrolet to families of estate labourers on their jaunts. Among others was the well-spoken retired English planter, boycotted by his peers as he set up home with his laundryman's daughter. He often called on me at the Kachcheri to find some way of ensuring that his lady-love would inherit the impressive house he had built on government leased land. One cannot forget this strangely-matched couple driving into town in their immense Wolseley car, he in tailored tweeds and military moustache and she, a dark-eyed beauty, always in expensive finery. And then – there was the film star .....

We first met her thanks to one of our friends, a handsome rising star in Sinhala cinema, who came up on week-end to 'Himalaya'. He was surprised that we did not know that a legend of the silver screen had followed in Greta Garbo's footsteps, forsaken a glittering career, and opted for a family life of quiet obscurity in Aluth Eliya. Our investigations located her, married to an officer of the Provisions Department, living a bit out of town. After a friendly phone call from our friend, we were invited to call on her. We did so that very evening – and were overwhelmed by the lavish hospitality of our hostess. Over a decade had passed since she danced across the screen, in diaphanous costumes, as the heroine of a historical romance – but our now-matronly hostess yet showed glimpses of her legendary beauty, her flashing eyes and the winsome smile that had launched a thousand fan letters. Since then, we became friends and her invitations to dinner we gratefully accepted as her cuisine was superlative and a far, far cry from the stodgy concoctions of our awful bachelors' cook. The luxury of their home and the quality of hospitality was way beyond the income that could be earned by her husband, a genial host with a suave manner. We naively attributed their lavish life-style to his inherited wealth as scion of a minor 'walauwa'. It was some months later that rumours reached our ears of his underhand 'commissions' extracted to purchase poor quality goods from farmers.

Curfew

The hot winds of political turmoil began to be felt in Aluth Eliya. Its charmed existence began to crumble with the declaration of the very first national Emergency. An era, which had been symbolised by the Head of State driving up from Colombo preceded by a single Police motor-cyclist, was drawing to a turbulent close. Our good fortune was that none of us were political prophets with dark forebodings. No 'Emergency' could upset the carefree tenor of our life in 'Himalaya'. At a solemn conference of staff officers the Government Agent allocated us various specific 'security' responsibilities and most significantly, Curfew Passes which gave us, and our cars, the authority to be any where at any time. (Little did I ever imagine that I would be going the same task myself, a decade and a half later, in a Kachcheri by the sea!). These Passes rapidly became status symbols, and those of us who had them walked on air. Especially so, as Aluth Eliya was yet favoured by the gods who spared it from any disturbance – and our capacity for crisis management was thus never put to the test.

Our Curfew Passes, however, became an essential adjunct to the moveable feast of 'curfew parties' that quietly flourished during this dismal period. Dinners and sing-songs were held at various homes, where the young blood from 'Himalaya' were always welcome, not merely for our bonhomie and singing but also as duly authorised transporters of 'pass-less' guests. A favoured venue was the home of a senior doctor and his English wife. The music, cuisine and company were of exemplary quality – especially so as some guests were among the few of our acquaintances who had foreign wives who were often amused at the cheeky irreverence of our conversation. There was the greying engineer, scapegrace son of a senior judge, who had been packed off to England many years ago so that his escapades would not disgrace his father. He had come back to Ceylon with his Scots wife, long after his father's demise, to seek his fortune in his homeland. He had a fund of yarns of which the most memorable was his account of the legendary Bracegirdle with whom he shared pints at his neighbourhood pub. What tickled both of them was that our friend's father had been on the Bench that extradited that anti-colonial 'subversive' from this corner of Empire! Another was a local padre with his Welsh wife he had met when he was pastor in a remote coal-mining community. He seemed to have lost his standing there after he took to wife one of their daughters, and had returned to pursue his calling in his homeland. His home was popular in town as he ran a favourite lodging house for young working girls. Once in a while the bluff Burgher police chief deigned to drop in for dinner and tried to send shivers down our spines with tales of marauding mobs likely to invade the bazaar, caches of hidden bombs and so on. Tales too tall to believe – so we mistakenly thought.

The Bomb

During this period of murder and mayhem elsewhere, life flowed on placidly in our little town. Or so it did till The Bomb Affair. One fine day our friend the Purchasing Officer, the film star's husband, rushed to the Police Station, dishevelled and panic-stricken. He had opened the front door to collect the newspaper only to discover a large and sinister-looking parcel, addressed to him, on his doorstep. He was sure that it was a parcel bomb – and rushed out via the back-door to seek Police help. The Police chief had been longing for just such an opportunity to test the, much-rehearsed but never yet tested, bomb disposal techniques of his policemen. He put his plan into action. Meanwhile, the sensational news had travelled fast in town – and quite a bandwagon followed the Police jeep and its posse of armed constables. They gingerly stepped out of the jeep when they reached .the 'scene of the crime'. The 'film-star' in hysterics, had sought refuge, meanwhile, in a neighbour's home.

The policemen, watched by the curious crowd, with their rifles ready, advanced on the verandah where the suspect parcel could be seen To our puzzlement, in the forefront of the squad was a shabbily dressed man inexplicably carrying a long fishing rod. The Officer-in-Charge, 'leading' from the rear like all good generals, enlightened us. The mystery man was the Police "sanitary cooly" conscripted as expendable cannon-fodder! As we watched the poor 'fisherman' – after many unsuccessful tries – managed to hook the parcel. Carrying the rod with its unconventional catch, he led a straggling line of police riflemen on to a vacant playground. The parcel was nervously deposited and the police formed a cautiously distant semicircle crouching with their rifles aimed at it. At the O.I.C's stentorian command 'Fire!' the rifles spat fire and an impressive volley deafened us.

But, to everybody's puzzlement, there was no explosion. When the gunsmoke cleared we saw that the suspect parcel had been blown to smithereens and its remains surrounded by many snake-like, but inert, objects. The policemen nervously advanced led, as usual, by the cooly. As he reached the 'snakes' he burst into a loud hoot of laughter and grabbed a handful of – dogs' tails! The suppliers of provisions, unable to tolerate our friend's increasing demands for 'cuts', had sent him a clear message and ensured maximum publicity .... The film star disappeared from us as rapidly as a shooting (!) star.

THE DUKE OF MONTE MISTO

Little did I imagine that I would soon be rubbing shoulders with a blue-blooded Duke when my chief, the Government Agent of Aluth Eliya where I was a District Land Officer, instructed me to inspect Monte Misto Estate to assess its suitability to be acquired by government in order to settle landless Kandyan peasants. This was in the post-1956 era when the government strove to undo the damage wreaked by the Colonial Waste Lands Ordinance which had evicted the forefathers of these peasants from their ancestral lands, driving them into landless penury. As I jolted down the rugged surface, hairpin bends and dizzying slopes of the road down to Monte Misto, I was struck by the poetic justice that it was the lot of the last British Government Agent to give back to these peasants the lands his predecessors in office had grabbed from their ancestors. I had by now become attuned to the hazards of driving down this precipitous road. Warned by raucous honking I nervously edged into a minuscule layby whenever a lorry laden with vegetables chugged past marketwards leaving behind an aroma of fresh greens, or an estate tractor crawled along with a ripe load of manure. A more interesting encounter was on wedding days when I crossed paths with a magnificent scarlet Chevrolet bulging with delightfully tipsy estate women draped in sarees of blinding brightness. Their chauffeur was a legend in Aluth Eliya – a burly, tanned "European" in a rakish cowboy hat. This was Mr. Colt, a once wealthy Eurasian, who had wined and womanised away his patrimony and cheerfully descended to chauffeuring his one-time workers on their jaunts in his limousine. He was also known to claim that one of his granduncles was the man who developed the legendary Colt revolver, the weapon of choice in America's wild West.

Monte Misto

As I rounded the last bend and came within sight of Monte Misto Estate it became abundantly clear that its owner would never fight to retain ownership. Accustomed as I was to the neatly barbered tea bushes and well maintained line rooms of the best estates, the seedy decrepitude of my destination was a sad surprise. An expanse of straggly tea bushes, battling it out with weeds, sloped upwards past sad clusters of ramshackle line rooms to vegetable plots clinging to steep slopes. A slow chugging could be heard from the estate's little factory and, surprisingly, an incongruous little chapel like building could be seen, empty and forlorn. I looked around for the Superintendent's Bungalow, usually perched on the most scenic spot on the estate, but saw no signs of one. At last I found the crazily tilted signpost which pointed me in the right direction. The bungalow was tucked away in a little dell, out of sight from the tea, the line rooms and the factory.

After the desolation of the estate, the bungalow was a totally unexpected sight. It was a scaled down English manor, straight from the illustrated historical romances of my boyhood. Walls of weathered red brick, bay windows wreathed in climbing honeysuckle, and an elegant porch emblazoned with a coat of arms. As I drove up in my dusty car, I was greeted with a firm handshake by a rotund Englishman with twinkling blue eyes, Mr. Charles Coultsleigh, the owner. "Don't you think, young man, that one's home has to be far removed from one's place of work ? It's essential for one's peace of mind. That's why my grandfather built this house, almost hidden from the estate but comfortingly near enough to handle any crisis. I always felt sorry for station-masters and postmasters perched on top of their workplaces". We were chatting over a delicious cup of tea served, to my surprise, by a demure damsel in a 'lama sari ' – not the expected white shirted Tamil 'boy'. With a hearty guffaw he said, with disarming frankness, "This tea is from my friend Hugh in High Forest. Monte Misto tea is now so ghastly I wouldn't serve it to my worst enemy ! We can talk more at lunch, after we walk around the estate – whose new owner you'll be – poor boy !" he said with another guffaw.

The Field Inspection

Walking round Monte Misto with its owner was both a most depressing and extraordinarily interesting experience. It was depressing to walk the overgrown paths bordered by neglected tea bushes and see the listless labourers gloomily lounging outside their ramshackle line-rooms. Their demeanour showed no great confidence in the young officer in whose hands their future lay. The mere thought of burdening my shoulders with this multitude of problems appalled me. Coultsleigh, on the other hand, was extraordinarily cheery – for the very same reason. He was ridding himself of a white elephant ... He kept up a running commentary as we trudged along. "That chapel looking building was built long ago to be a church. But it never got going. The itinerant pastor, whose 'parish' covered many estates had no luck with the Tamil labourers here who stood loyally by their little Hindu shrines that dotted the place. He also made a silly mistake when he arrived to take possession, but accompanied by a man carrying an empty coffin – to be filled by any future convert who wished burial in hallowed ground. A most inauspicious start, poor chap. It was never consecrated, and has remained empty since then."

We were shown round the little hydro-powered factory by a red-eyed tea maker, clearly alcohol-powered judging from the aroma that surrounded him. The steep upper slopes of little vegetable plots that the labourers were allowed to cultivate had kept them going during the estate's slow decline.

Revelations

And so to lunch. Our hostess was another surprise to me. Instead of the expected 'memsahib' I was welcomed with a 'namaskare' by a plump and smiling Kandyan 'Kumarihamy' in traditional 'osariya'. "Meet my wife Leela. Her father was the Nilame of the Elakande Devale. She's been to the Convent – but refuses to speak English to my guests" said my host with a wry smile. After some pleasant small talk in Sinhala, we sat down to a truly Kandyan repast while our hostess busied herself in seeing that the young 'menike' kept our plates piled high.

My host was reluctant to let me go as he sensed in me a sympathetic ear to his conversation. He invited me to his library to join him for coffee. It was a cosy little place with bookshelves carrying an odd mix of old leather bound classics and dog-eared paperbacks reflecting the varying tastes of the last few decades. Above the trophy laden mantlepiece, of a rarely used fireplace, hung the portrait in oils of a formally dressed Victorian Englishman in mutton-chop whiskers, painted with the shadowy background of a tea plantation. Coultsleigh chuckled as he saw me looking curiously at the picture. "That's my grandfather who came out from England, when Victoria was queen, to open up a tea plantation here. The best lands had long been taken and he had to be satisfied with the shrub covered hill he found here. Villagers called it 'Meedum Kanda ' – Hill of Mists. Grandfather was an avid reader of Alexandre Dumas whose 'Count of Monte Cristo' enthralled him. He therefore gave his land the exotic name of 'Monte Misto'."

With a twinkle in his eye he asked me "Did you cross a red Chevrolet on your way here ?" I nodded 'yes'. "That was my brother Bill". "But you are Coultsleigh and he is Colt" I puzzled. "After Bill ran through the wealth our father had left him, he felt that he should not bring dishonour to the family name and decided to call himself Colt – even claiming relationship to an American gunsmith! I am fond of him, but he discreetly keeps his distance, so as not to embarrass me. He's gentleman enough for that".

As I rose to leave, Coultsleigh walked me up to the porch. "Did you see the family coat of arms up there ?" he pointed out to a carving of two mythical animals holding up a shield emblazoned with strange devices. "That's a long story that can await your next field inspection. But you'd better hurry back before the road gets covered by the evening mists of Meedum Kanda".

A Ducal Heritage

Over the next few months, I paid many field visits to Monte Misto to work out the nitty-gritty details of listing assets, surveying the land, counting resident labour and other mind-numbing tasks. Coultsleigh always insisted I lunch with him. I was a willing guest and a fascinated listener as, during the many weeks of our association, he regaled me with the saga of the lost dukedom of Coultsleigh he was heir to.

Everard Fortescue, the grandfather whose portrait graced the library, was the third son of the eighth Duke of Coultsleigh in Sussex. His eldest brother led the fox hunting, grouse shooting life of the ruling class, biding his time to succeed to his father's dukedom in the fullness of time. The second brother went into the army to fight the many wars that spread the Queen's Empire over the globe. Everard decided against accepting a tame bishopric that was within the Duke's demesne. He preferred to seek his fortune planting tea in distant Ceylon. He sailed here with his young bride Catherine.

Roughing it out in the wilderness of Meedum Kanda, while Everard slogged away at taming the wilderness, took a heavy toll on poor Catherine's health. She gave birth to a baby boy and passed away soon after. Everard sent his baby son back to England with a kind-hearted planter's family going back on furlough. While he wrested tea from an unyielding soil, he saw no need to burden himself with another delicate English rose allergic to the tropic air. Following a well-established tradition, he shared his bed with a succession of dusky damsels from his work force. Meanwhile Algernon, the son he had sent to England, grew up under the benign neglect of his grandfather the Duke. At the appropriate age he went to Harrow and was on the verge of going up to Oxford, when his father summoned him back to Ceylon and Monte Misto so that he could prepare himself, in due course, to take over the running of the estate.

Julia Cameron, the pioneer woman photographer of the Victorian era, once lived up in High Forest Estate owned by the Cameron

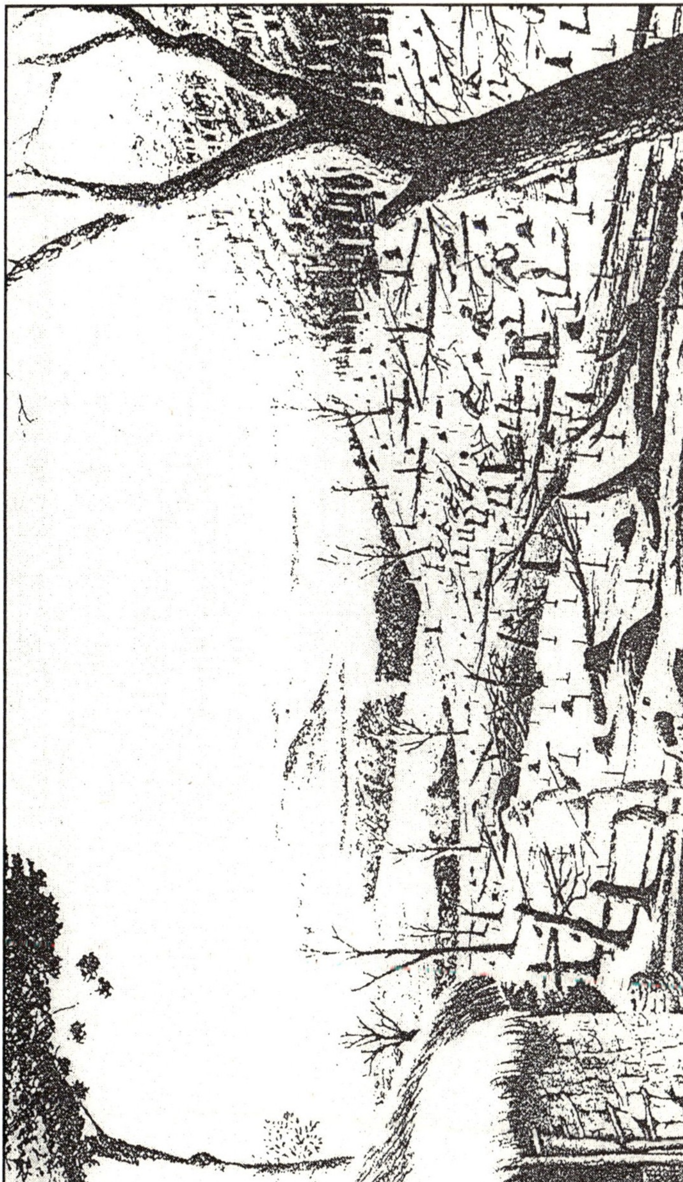

Wrested tea from unyielding soil

family. Among her photographs is one of a young Everard posing stiffly in planter's mufti while a pale and visibly wilting Catherine smiles wistfully at Julia's strange contraption. A long low thatched roof house can be glimpsed in the dim background.

Algernon and Sons

In the fullness of time old Everard passed away while up at Aluth Eliya for the horse races. His tombstone in the churchyard of Holy Trinity Church records that he was the youngest son of the Duke of Coultsleigh. Algernon now buckled down to the task of running Monte Misto. He was a good planter and a solid citizen. He managed to make Monte Misto a paying, though not very, proposition. He shied away from dalliances with native wenches and went on to marry Mary Green, the "white" daughter of an English planter and his resident Tamil mistress. Green never married Mary's mother. Liaisons were accepted, paternal responsibility appreciated but marriage to a "native coolie" was "just not done, old boy" in his milieu of Edwardian planterdom. He acknowledged Mary as his daughter, saw to her lady-like Convent education and gave her away in marriage, will ill-concealed pride, to Algernon, a true-blue Englishman.

Algernon never went back to England. He may have cringed at the prospect of introducing a wife with "a touch of the tar brush" to ducal company. But he was proud of his noble ancestry and lost no opportunity to din it into his sons Charles and William. They were never to forget that in their background was Algernon's grandfather the Duke who claimed descent through a tortuous route, among bypaths littered with barons, earls and counts, from a bastard (but acknowledged and ennobled) daughter of England's rakehell King Charles II.

Algernon's sons Charles and William were boarded at Trinity College, Kandy. Their father wanted them to be fully integrated into Ceylon life so that they would not have to undergo the painful readjustment that he had to suffer when he was pitchforked from

Harrow and the ducal mansion to the wilderness of Monte Misto. Both sons excelled in school, Charles in his studies and William in rugby. Their father decided to send Charles to the Oxford he had missed, and began training William to take over the estate.

Charles spent his vacations with his great-grandfather the old Duke, now quite doddering and living out the tail end of his life in his decaying mansion. He never seemed very sure as to the identity of the young great-grandson who visited him, but treated him with unfailing courtesy. His oldest son, heir to the dukedom, had died after being thrown by his horse while out fox-hunting. The son next in line, supposed to be soldiering away in the Army, was somewhere in "the Empire where the sun never set". The old Duke seemed to have only the haziest recollection of Everard in Ceylon and none whatsoever of Algernon. Charles had a great time at Oxford which he left with a "gentleman's degree" but no regrets. He was popular with the few Ceylonese undergrads there, scions of the local aristocracy. Among them was the man destined to be our Prime Minister.

William, to his father's great disappointment, proved to be an indifferent planter more interested in the rugby, cricket and dances at planters' clubs than in developing the estate. Algernon died an unhappy man. In the course of his carefree carousing career William ran through the assets his father had left him. In desperation he sent an SOS to Charles, now a high executive in an Agency House. Charles decided to give up his lucrative position and make an attempt to rescue Monte Misto. He bought up William's share leaving him to roister, with democratic glee, surrounded by willing lasses from village and estate.

Charles Takes Over

Charles found, to his dismay, that running an estate hands-on was a far cry from supervising it from an Agency House in Colombo. It was a run-down patrimony that he had quixotically taken over. He made a strenuous effort to resuscitate it after William's depredations and, at long last, made it a paying proposition once again. Perhaps inspired by the same liberal ideas he had imbibed at Oxford, as was his distinguished contemporary, Charles quietly established excellent relations with the people of the Sinhala villages that surrounded the estate. These people had been absolutely ignored by his father and grandfather whose social vision had been bounded by their Tamil workforce and fellow planters. In a way, William had laid the foundation with his indiscriminate love life. But Charles was an Oxonian gentleman. He moved with the great and good of the villages – monks, teachers and Village Headmen – and soon became an honoured guest at local functions – school prize-givings, temple functions and such where he polished up his rudimentary Sinhala.

A frequent presence at these functions was the Nilame's pretty daughter, whom the old man brought along to translate his conversations with Charles. It didn't take long for the two young people to fall in love. It was Colonial Ceylon and the old Nilame sensed that an English son-in-law would be a tremendous asset. But he was Buddhist enough to insist that it could never be a church wedding. Charles' loyalty to the faith of his fathers had been badly eroded at liberal Oxford. So the wedding was a grand Sinhala affair, but cold-shouldered by Charles' fellow English planters. However, Charles was now a respected and accepted member of the village 'establishment', and it was a happy, though sadly childless, marriage.

The Lost Dukedom

Back in England the old Duke had died, a senile centenarian, leaving no records of his heirs, if any. World War II was raging when the College of Heralds and/or Debrett's Peerage published notices calling for claimants to the dukedom. Charles never saw them. He later learnt that they had received information from Kenya that Everard's older brother had ended up as white farmer, but died childless. "So, you see young man, you have been talking to the rightful, though last, Duke of Coultsleigh ! I can't be bothered dragging my unwilling Kumarihamy to ghastly post-war Britian to reclaim my heritage, put on a silly coronet and sit in the House of Lord. So here I am."

The acquisition of the estate went tickety-boo. The usual haggling over the quantum of compensation never took place. To my considerable surprise the Government Valuer tamely accepted the owner's, Charles', grossly inflated claim. Charles "laughed all the way to the Bank" while I 'inherited' Monte Misto.

To the House of Lords

Some months later I received an embossed invitation to a reception at Kandy's Queen's Hotel to felicitate Charles Coultsleigh on his elevation to the Senate of Ceylon. In keeping with his conciliatory policies, our Prime Minister had nominated his old friend from Oxford to be the 'token white' in the Senate !

It was a glittering reception for the great and good, the rich and famous .... not quite my scene. But as soon as he saw me, the Senator welcomed me with a bear hug. He introduced me to all and sundry. "This is the young man who made me a millionaire – by buying my Monte Misto". He then drew me to a quiet corner and said "You deserve to hear the rest of my story. I met old Banders (you know who) at the annual Oxford dinner in Colombo. As I grumbled about the travails of running my estate he asked me whether I was prepared to sell it to government. He was looking for land on which to settle landless villagers. I was more than willing, but lay no great store by a politician's promises after a dinner flowing with wine. So I could not believe my eyes when you landed on my doorstep, a few weeks later, and wanted to take my white elephant into your hands ! I must thank you, young Tissa, for that good deed as well as for listening to my yarns of my ancestors. You must write it down some time. It's a good story, but please wait till this last Duke is no more. You should never forget that, after all, though I did not take my seat in the House of Lords at Westminster the rightful Duke of Coultsleigh did make it to the Upper House of his chosen homeland, Ceylon!"

THE HOUSE OF BUDDHIST CURTAINS

"Are you Buddhists ?" asked the old lady who had advertised her house in Nuwara Eliya for rent. "Yes" we admitted with some nervousness as her hall bristled with many objects and pictures proclaiming her Christian piety. "Then you'll be very happy with the curtains" she said. We were so overjoyed by her acceptance as tenants that we did not try to work out what she meant.

House-hunting

We were newly married and looking for a place in Nuwara Eliya to set up house. Chasing a classified Ad we located Mrs. Bimgoda down a gloomy pathway lined with uncut grass, untrimmed shrubs, shadowed by dark old trees – an unlikely cul-de-sac off up-market Ward Place. The house was old, sprawling and decrepit. An old car under the porch was being repaired by a blue-eyed man in greasy clothes who gestured us in with a wave of his oil-stained hand. Mrs. Bimgoda emerged from the inner darkness and invited us into her dimly lit parlour. She was a tall and elegant lady in Kandyan saree. Her carefully groomed hair was all white but her face yet bore the remains of youthful beauty. The parlour walls, side tables and whatnots were crowded with formal old group photographs in elaborate frarmes. On an easel there stood her wedding picture, every inch the radiant Kandyan bride, with her groom paunchy in Nilame's garb and a luxuriant moustache. We soon learnt that Mr. Bimgoda had passed away many years ago. In his heyday he had been a Rate Mahatmaya (R.M) who held sway in the Kandyan Provinces. The group photographs commemorated official farewells to the Bimgodas flanked by a chohort of Village Headmen in Bandoliers (crimson sashes); or to white topeed British Government Agents, and their memsahibs, flanked by R.M. Bimgoda and his peers in Kandyan garb, all sporting bushy moustaches and/or flourishing sideburns.

Mrs. Bimgoda was every inch the lady in our business palaver. The deal was briskly concluded on the usual N'Eliya terms. During "The Season" we were to move into the little annexe leaving the main house free for holiday makers from Colombo who paid handsomely for this toehold in the hills. As our new landlady accompanied us to the veranda she gestured towards a few pathetic piles of old woolen clothes laid out for sale, and shyly said "You may find these useful. It does get chilly up there!" We mumbled our regrets and made a quick getaway.

No.3 Buttercup Drive

Driving into N'Eliya my wife was enthralled by the green sward of the golf links, the soughing of the wind in the fir trees, the scent of pine resin and the quaint houses with gables and bay-windows. What a place to start a new life ! Her enthusiasm rapidly petered out when we came to No.3 Buttercup Drive whose tenants we had become.

It was a long narrow house with a red "takaran" roof. No paint brush had touched its walls for many years. No holly hocks, lilies, roses or buttercups brightened the garden. Instead leeks, carrots and radishes sprouted from the black soil of carefully tended beds. Far down the garden stood a shabby little hut of planks with its fragile roof weighted with rocks and tyres against the howling winds of monsoon months. A squat and weather-beaten old lady emerged from its low doorway, bundled in several layers of moth eaten woollen garments, a muffler tightly wound round her ears. She was the caretaker. She squinted at our letter of authority laboriously scrawled by Mrs. Bimgoda and satisfied herself of our bona-fides. A key was extracted from the inner recesses of her garments and she ushered us into our new home. My wife stepped across the threshold with a longing backward look at the gnarled old peach tree laden with fruit that stood at our doorstep. Alas! It was forbidden fruit in terms of our tenancy.

The Buddhist Curtains

Our house was no pseudo-Tudor cottage with mullioned windows and a fire place for pine logs. It was instead, a purpose built dormitory. A central corridor, with bed rooms on either side, led from living room to dining room. Every door and window had curtains, all sagging sadly from old twine strung from nail to nail. One look at the curtains and we understood the significance of Mrs. Bimgoda's question about our religion. They were printed all over with pictures of a Japanese Buddha! Buddhas galore – printed right side up, upside down and any old way, interspersed with parasols, Fujiyama and cherry blossoms ! Obviously produced by Japanese in the immediate post-war years for sale to Buddhists in South and South East Asia – whose consumer "tastes" had never been properly researched. We were horror-struck by Mrs. Bimgoda's unwitting sacrilege and rapidly took down all her valued curtains, storing them for re-hanging when holiday makers took over from us. The doors and windows where our "Buddhist curtains" once hung were now draped with an unmatching medley of hangings extracted post-haste from parental homes.

As the months went by we adjusted to our new life in N'Eliya. The house in Buttercup Drive turned out to be quite cosy in spite of its shabby exterior and tatty furniture. The tough – seeming caretaker was a sweet old thing who took my wife under her wing. She commandeered the kitchen and proved herself a superb cook although encumbered by a snotty little grandson clinging to her knees, cocooned in layers of grimy sweaters reminiscent of the street urchins of Dickensian London.

On our occasional forays to Colombo we always paid a courtesy call on Mrs. Bimgoda. Every time we visited her the same mechanic was around puttering with yet another old car. We presumed him to be a lodger in outer room and never gave him much thought.

The Arrival of John Smith

Came "The Season". We hurriedly removed our own hangings and restrung the "Buddhist curtains" just as they had always been. Our temporary residence was the little annexe. We adjusted to the loud cheeriness and high jinks of the holiday-makers in the main house and took stock of our new "home". We were fascinated. It was a microcosm of a bygone era, cramped with quaintly carved furniture upholstered in now-tattered velvet and numerous framed photographs documenting the life and times of the Bimgodas. These were informal and far different from the formal group photographs exhibited in Mrs. Bimgoda's drawing-room in Ward Place. We were both interested and intrigued trying to work out who was who – and never quite succeeded. Mrs. Bimgoda had been a stunningly beautiful bride in her wedding portrait. R.M. Bimgoda had been quite a bit older than her, paunchy and stolid but looking as pleased as punch to have married such a beauty. They had been photographed at the Nuwara Eliya races, the Flower Show, Hakgala Gardens and at the Governor's reception at Queen's Cottage. A fascinating window into colonial Ceylon.

There were also a few much older pictures which made us doubt Mrs. Bimgoda's Kandyan origins. One was of a solemn little baby girl seated on the lap of her mother who was dressed in a long dress with puffed sleeves with the father standing behind in a sherwani buttoned all the way. Another was of this girl, now older, in her confirmation dress on the steps of St. Lucia's Cathedral, Kotahena. Could this be of our landlady in her childhood ? Who had she been ? But what really puzzled us were the host of pictures of the Bimgodas with a distinctly European looking baby boy whose steady progress had been lovingly preserved in these photographs. In the earliest photograph a tubby little boy, about one year old, uneasily clutched the hands of the two Bimgodas. Behind them we could discern, partly obscured, the building and signboard of a well-known orphanage for "Eurasian" babies, poor little unwanted children of white planters who had fathered them on "native" women. It was obvious that the childless Bimgodas had formally adopted one of these bonny blue eyed babies. His growing up was faithfully recorded – playing with dogs and servant boy; first day at school in cap, boots and satchel; in Boy Scout uniform and finally in the rugger team of a famous school in Kandy. At last we found his name – on a class prize certificate for "Handicraft". It was John Smith. Clearly the Bimgodas in colonial Ceylon had been bucked no end to adopt a blue eyed "European" boy. So we thought at the time. I wondered where he now was. My wife claimed to see a faint resemblance between the teenage rugger player and the blue eyed mechanic always puttering around cars in Mrs. Bimgoda's garden. I pooh-poohed her as I could not believe that such a lovingly nurtured boy could sink that far.

Historical Research

My parents joined the holiday trek up country to stay with us, incidentally checking out the domestic competence of their new daughter-in-law. They were fascinated by our cramped little annexe awash with mementoes of the Bimgodas. As a scholar of bygone ages Father scrutinised the photographs to identify the various notables from their locales and the buildings in the background. Mother was taken up with observing the dated women's fashions pictured, of the good ladies of R.M's, Disawas and Mudaliyars as well of Colonial memsahibs, wives of Govt. Agents, Police Superintendents and the like.

After the mandatory evening stroll along pine scented walks and a slap-up dinner we sat around huddled in Mrs. Bimgoda's cosily padded armchairs comfortably chatting away. As she examined the photographs Mother gave a delighted shriek of recognition. "Daddy, isn't this the famous Ivy Rodrigo?" We looked over her shoulder at a studio portrait of a young and stunningly beautiful Mrs. Bimgoda, not in Kandyan saree but in a long and elegant frock. After a careful scrutiny Father agreed with the identification. "It's Ivy all right, around the time of her great escapade".

R. M. Bimgoda, Ivy and little John

Burning with curiosity we clamoured for an explanation. We just could not imagine our decorous and dignified landlady being involved in an adventure of any sort. But we soon learnt that things are never what they seem. After some gentle persuasion Mother told the story of what had been dubbed the "scandal of the Century" in Colonial Ceylon.

The Scandal

Ivy Alles had been the beautiful daughter of a prosperous liquor wholesaler in Kotahena. Her sumptuous wedding at St. Lucia's Cathedral to the eminent physician Dr. Tony Rodrigo filled many columns of the "Morning Leader". Soon after his marriage Dr. Rodrigo received the accolade of being appointed Physician-in-Attendance to H.E the Governor of Ceylon. The Rodrigos were honoured by an invitation to the Governor's Levee at Queen's House to honour the King's Birthday. The "creme de la creme" of colonial society was there in full panoply puffed with loyal pride. This crowd of "native gentry" was unobtrusively managed by a handful of British A.D.C's – Public School youths of good pedigree and impeccable manners.

Tallest and most handsome of this cohort was Roland Smythe. As his blue eyes met Ivy Rodrigo's black eyes across the crowded lawn there flared the lightning of true passion. They stood next to each other, entranced and almost speechless, while voices chattered and cutlery clattered around them. Their fates was sealed. Assignations were far from easy in staid Colombo. "Society" was a tight little circle. They could not meet in either of Colombo's two hotels or its sole Tea Room (as cafes were then called). However, the lovers did manage to meet, though nobody yet knows how. But an inter-racial romance, adulterous to boot, just could not be concealed for long. Sly observations led to whispers, whispers led inevitably to the national pastime of anonymous petitions to the Governor and the betrayed husband.

The Governor acted first and fast. Roland Smythe was held

incommunicado in Queen's House until he was bundled into the next P& O liner to Britain, his career in tatters. Ivy fled her sullied marital home back to her parents. Unable to face the stigma of her conduct the Alles family quietly packed her off, with a generous endowment, to an up country convent where she could ponder her folly.

Poor cuckolded Dr. Rodrigo had his marriage annulled, at great cost, and took up a post in the Colonial Medical Service in Malaya. Nothing more was heard of Ivy.

The Transformation of Ivy

Four keen and curious minds had no difficulty in piecing together the rest of the story by intelligent conjecture and photographic evidence. Ivy had given birth to a blue-eyed boy in some obscure hospital. The infant boy had then been presented to the well-known orphanage for Eurasian children. The coming together of RM Bimgoda and Ivy can only be conjectured. Bimgoda, the rural laird would have been in N'Eliya to report to his European Asst. Govt. Agent. Rambling alone amidst pine-shaded walks he would have been struck by the pale beauty of Ivy with her down cast eyes. When he shyly spoke, her eyes lit up at the prospect of an honourable escape from the convent walls – and more. A quiet wedding in a little up-country chapel attended only by his rural kinsfolk kept them out of society's limelight.

An year or two passed. No little Bimgodas were produced to cheer the R.M's heart. Ivy then unobtrusively guided his footsteps towards the Eurasian orphan's home. There she singled out little blue-eyed "John Smith" to be their adopted son. An extraordinarily adroit move by Ivy to reclaim her son by Roland Smythe. Old Bimgoda, ruling his hills and wilds, seems to have been supremely unaware of the tragic love story whose unwitting dupe he had become.

Farewell to the Hills

Not long after, the transfer list moved us from the misty hills of Nuwara Eliya to the vast reservoirs and sacred sites of Anuradhapura. We left our house of Buddhist curtains with a bit of nostalgia and a tantalising tale to tell. But we looked forward to the spacious official bungalow we were scheduled to occupy. Blue eyed Smith was yet meddling with a broken down car when we paid our farewell to Mrs. Bimgoda – whom we now looked upon with awe befitting Helen of Troy!

The Truth

A few weeks ago newspapers carried the following obituary notice:

"The death is announced of Mrs. Ivy Bimgoda,
relict of Rate Mahattaya Bimgoda;
mother of John Smith ... ..."
The truth, acknowledged ... ... at last.

A TALE OF THE SEA

THE MERMAID'S BRACELET

Grandpa Lloyd ran off to sea as a cabin boy about 120 years ago. Colombo harbour was a smaller and friendlier place in those far-off days. Boys on their way back from school in Mutwal enjoyed hanging on jetty railings to stare wide-eyed at ships and sailors of all shapes and colours as they came alongside in launches or 'bum boats' and rushed off to paint the town red. One day young Lloyd saw a poster on the notice board saying "Wanted : Cabin Boy. Ship sailing tomorrow. Apply to Agent". Lloyd was thrilled at the idea of chucking up school and sailing the seven seas. He met the ship agent and captain, lied about his age, and .... got the job! He was due to sail the very next day and cleverly planned his getaway from home and school. Next morning he set off for school as usual, but also carried a small parcel of clothes. On his way he stopped off at the jetty, gave his books to his best friend with strict instructions to return them to Lloyd's parents some days later and confess the truth, by which time he would be safe on the high seas. Everything went tickety-boo. Lloyd, the unwilling student, sailed away to a lifetime on board the ships he loved so much. His parents were bereft but helpless. Several years were to pass before Lloyd's ship touched Colombo again and his parents saw him as a seasoned young sailor who brought them loads of gifts to make belated amends for his great escape. He spent a lifetime at sea, on merchant ships that sailed the world's oceans. During World War I he served on a Royal Navy minesweeper and won a medal he proudly framed for posterity. His last sea-going assignment was on the coastal steamer "Lady Blake" that sailed from Colombo to Batticaloa.

By the time we grandchildren got to know him he had retired to his farmyard, within hearing distance of the sea. He was surrounded by a menagerie of poultry, cute bantam fowls, gobbling turkeys, strange little guinea fowls and a squawking cockatoo. He spent his leisure whittling away with a sharp knife all sorts of fascinating things – dolls' furniture, a lotus of layered coconut shells, a pipe rack for Father and walking sticks with grotesque heads. He chewed tobacco sliced from a plug of oozy black stuff, looking deceptively like 'kalu dodol' – as we found to our cost. I remember him giving us the most plausible explanation for the roll of thunder "Putha, those are the gods playing marbles in heaven!"

The Girl on the Rock

Like all sailors in pirate yarns, Grandpa's arms were tattooed. The left forearm carried the enchanting figure of a mermaid, the other a rampant cobra. On the wrist of his right (cobra) arm he always wore a bracelet, twisted, black and strangely gleaming. We never saw him without it. When he came to 'baby-sit' me during a long convalescence from a childhood illness he entertained me by relating the story behind the tattoos and bracelet. It was so enthralling that it yet echoes down the years, and I remember it well enough to relate it to my own grandchildren.

"Our ship was sailing across the Atlantic, from Brazil to South Africa, when it developed some engine trouble. Luckily we were not too far away from St.Henry, a lonely and rarely visited island in mid-ocean. We limped into its little harbour and the captain set about the difficult task of repairing the engines in a poorly equipped little place with no electricity and few skilled workers. But he did get the job going and the sleepy old place began to echo to the sound of hammering on steel and the spluttering cough of engines being tested. Repairs took many days leaving most of us sailors with nothing to do. The town was a cold and windy place. Its people were gloomy and unfriendly, unused to the horseplay of bored young sailors fooling around and getting drunk in the town's only tavern. All this did not interest me and I took to wandering around St.Henry, which was only a very small island with nobody living away from the harbour. One windy evening as I walked along a lonely beach I thought I heard a woman's voice sweetly singing. I quietly walked towards the seaside rocks from where the singing came. To my astonishment, in the fading light I made out the figure of a young woman seated on a rock with her feet in the waves, quietly singing a strange song. As I went closer a strong fishy smell wafted over me. She was startled when I stepped on a broken shell with a loud crack, then looked at me with a gentle smile and said "Come closer, young man, but not too close". I did as I was told, wary of the sea serpent at the foot of the rock.

"Who are you ? What brings you to my island ?" I told her I was from Ceylon, a larger island in the warm tropical seas far, far away. Wistfully she said "That's too far for me to swim". I wondered what she meant and said she could always come by ship. With a tinkling laugh she said "Can't you see who I am ? I am a mermaid ! Come closer, I have something for you, my friend from the tropics". I thought she was joking, but yet went closer in the fading light. She stretched out her hand with something in it. "Take this" she said "Wear it all your life and you will be safe from storms, shipwrecks and disasters on land". I took a bracelet from her tingling fingers, and slipped it on. "Good bye, sailor from Ceylon. Never forget me !" and she dove into the waves with a swish of her fishtail that I now saw for the first, and last, time in my life."

Grandpa's story was like a dream as I drifted in and out of sleep during my convalescence. As time went on, it remained only a vague memory. We went far away to another town. Studying the atlas for geography I remembered Grandpa's story of the island of St.Henry – but never found it in any map.

Grandpa passed away peacefully a few years later. I stood by his body, neatly dressed in his naval uniform for the last time. My eyes went to his wrist where his strange bracelet yet remained. Strangely, it had completely lost the magical gleam that had so fascinated me. It was now a dull, dead, black.

RETURN TO TRINCOMALEE

THE CURIOUS HUNT FOR MARUSINGHE

Whenever I recall that fateful night of April 1971 at China Bay where echoes in my mind's ear a poem from my school days "The Night before Waterloo" – a dream of fair women and brave men dancing at a ball on the eve of battle. An immense hangar at the airfield was aflutter with bunting and balloons; fairy lights twinkled merrily and the Air Force band played romantic airs. It was Air Force Night. Gorgeously dressed women, outdone by their officer escorts in magnificent dress uniforms danced to lilting music. Among the distinguished guests was a wickedly handsome French diplomat escorting a lissom brown beauty in a micro-mini of gold mesh. A charming raconteur, he claimed to be the fourteenth Frenchman at the South Pole while frankly confessing he had flown – not slogged there on skis.

Clad in a nondescript lounge suit, swamped and outgunned by the gold braid, crimson, white and blue of service commanders I represented the civil administration as the Government Agent of Trincomalee District. Wine flowed, women danced and song resounded – a magnificent finale before the proud tower of complacent "stability" crumbled round our ears.

While revelry reigned fast and furious in the decorated hangar, the radioman in his lonely cabin listened aghast to the ominous message that crackled through his earphones. He scribbled it down and sent his orderly hot foot to the dance. The service commanders and I were loosely grouped together, cheerfully chatting, slightly removed from the youthful revels. With a great clatter of boots the radio orderly breathlessly rushed into our midst, saluted smartly and handed over a message to his commander. When he read it the commander gasped, his eyes popped and his luxuriant airforce moustache quivered. He steadied his nerves with a long gulp from the glass in his hand, took a deep breath and addressed us sombrely "Gentlemen, I have just received a very important message that concerns us all. Let's go into my office to discuss it". Puzzled and worried we trooped along behind him – the Navy Commander, the senior Army Officer, the Superintendent of Police and the G.A. Soon after we sat down, despatch riders from the Navy, Army and Police rushed in with identical messages. Police stations had been attacked, mutiny was suspected and the Insurgency of 1971 had been launched ! After a brief discussion, sharing of information and establishing lines of communication we dispersed to our respective headquarters, tense and gloomy. The revels quietly petered out as officers and men were withdrawn to strengthen defence establishments.

Emergency

A State of Emergency was declared with the Government Agent as Competent Authority over all civilian and service establishments. It was a tremendous responsibility, yet strangely exciting. Trinco was isolated from the rest of the country as roads were unsafe. The Air Force was our only "life line" to Colombo. A cargo ship in harbour was commandeered, in case personnel had to be evacuated. A few service vehicles managed to run the insurgent gauntlet, peppered by cross fire. I clearly recall debriefing a Military Policeman who said – "I escaped thanks to the Tarzan films of my boyhood. When a bush stirred ahead of me, I knew the sniper was pulling a string from somewhere else. So I fired in that direction and made my getaway!".

The sleepy old Kachcheri became a hive of abnormal hyper activity. Officials were detailed to requisition food and fuel. A rudimentary rationing scheme was put in place. All licensed firearms were requisitioned – including an enormous elephant shooting gun treasured by a retired English planter. As always, curfew passes became status symbols and it needed all the tact of my Asst. G.A. to say "No" to the suppliants and yet remain friends.

We also established a rudimentary "intelligence gathering" operation. All divisional officers passed on whatever information they collected – largely of Sinhala youth who had disappeared from their homes in colonization schemes, work places in government institutions or local schools. There was also the occasional red herring such as the European padre quietly investigated as a possible member of Italy's Red Brigade. The Navy too had its suspects. A leading insurgent set off from Jaffna to raise a mutiny in the Trinco Dockyard but was shot dead. A search for potential mutineers uncovered the sentry guarding the GA's Residency!

Marusinghe

Piecing together our scraps of "intelligence" revealed that the charismatic cadetting master of the Maha Vidyalaya – Marusinghe – had disappeared from school and hostel many days ago. Further probing established that he had unobtrusively indoctrinated selected schoolboys and embarked on a rigorous regime of physical training – including long swims in the open sea with his friend the naval mutineer, now shot dead ! As there was no road communication with the rest of the country it was unlikely Marusinghe had fled to join his fellow insurgents in his Southern home. It was assumed that he had taken to the jungle to gather a band of insurgents and attack security installations. Among the papers he had left behind in his hurried getaway was an interesting map hidden in a bundle of the Pyongyang Times. It was a diagram of the roads in town leading to "targets" with exact positions indicated by numbering lamp posts and other such simple fool proof indicators. I knew the GA was an "enemy" to the insurgents, but it was yet unnerving to find my Residency arrowed in this map as a specific target for attack.

The Hunt Begins

The investigators spared nobody. They even came to The Residency and hauled off the young teacher who was tutoring my son, as he had been a colleague of Marusinghe's at the Maha Vidyalaya. He was cleared after a brief interview and to my son's disappointment – resumed tutoring.

The first searches began at Abhayapura, A Sinhala suburb, home to many of Marusinghe's pupils. Timid parents, roused by the midnight knock, and their nervous teenage sons were questioned by Police and all likely hiding places searched. We drew a blank – no boys had disappeared, no Marusinghe appeared. As our patrol was about to leave they heard suspicious scrabbling sounds and whimpering from a well nearby. They rushed to it with torches and shotguns, cock sure that their suspect had got himself well and truly trapped. The torches focused on the yellow and angry eyes of a large wildcat fallen in while raiding poultry. Spitting and scratching, it was rescued from a watery death and locked up in the barred vault of the old Dutch Kachcheri. By morning we found it had clawed its way to freedom !

Our next tip-off was from Andankulam, not far from town, a settlement bordered by the Navy water works on one side and several rocky outcrops on the other. It was reported that dim lights and suspicious movements were seen at night from a cave among these rocks. The Navy suspected that Marusinghe may have planned to sabotage its water supply scheme and launched a search operation one morning. Late in the evening the heavily armed patrol returned to the Dockyard greeted by raucous laughter. Their leading seaman flaunted on his bayonet the trophy of their chase – a black brassiere! This was all they found, with a mat, lamp and cook pot in the first cave they searched after a classic belly crawl and a blood curdling bayonet charge. All caves they searched were free of humans and were the rank smelling shelters of wild animals. Stern questioning of the nervous informant by the Navy made him confess that his wife had eloped with a young neighbour. He had located their love nest in a

Trophy of the Hunt

cave. Planning sweet revenge he tipped off the Navy that Marusinghe had been seen in this neighbourhood. He led them to the cave expecting the Navy to go in with guns blazing, blowing the lovers to smithereens. But the lovers had left the cave and disappeared. The Navy drew a blank. The deserted husband earned a resounding slap – and Marusinghe remained at large.

More Sightings

The next report came from Seruvila, reached after an arduous voyage by launch. The local police had discovered a lonely jungle hut where, villagers reported, groups of young would-be-insurgents had met for indoctrination. Marusinghe was said to have been an occasional "visiting lecturer". A thorough search revealed a cache of pathetic cigarette-tin "bombs" – but no signs of recent occupancy. The bird had flown – if he had ever come this way.

More news came from Kantalai where the Sugar Corporation had a sizable managerial cadre of young graduates, some of whom counted Marusinghe as a friend who visited them. This was more than enough for the investigating Police Inspector who subjected them to a brutal and humiliating grilling which revealed nothing. I found these young men, badly battered and broken spirited, squatting in an open shed. I took them into my custody and bussed them off to a camp in Colombo before worse could befall. (Years later this policeman shot himself dead in spectacular fashion, to escape indictment for murdering a lawyer).

It was now presumed that Marusinghe had taken to the huge expanse of pathless jungle that stretched between the road to Colombo and the road to Anuradhapura. Mysterious movements were sighted on the distant jungle verges of Kantalai reservoir. An army patrol stealthily crept their way through the jungle to the suspect site – only to find a lonely band of migrant fishermen drying fish in their lean-to huts. No, they had seen no insurgents.

Meanwhile, when yarns were swapped in the Wardrooms and Service Messes Marusinghe quietly acquired the stature of the Elusive Pimpernel. He was never actually seen, nor had he ever really struck. But this was a period of suppressed panic when the very foundations of the state seemed to have been shaken – and the services felt exposed and vulnerable.

Secret Agents

Confusing and disturbing snippets of information came from strange sources. A naval reservist who had married a local girl, was a favourite fifth columnist. Dressed scruffily, and looking thoroughly "rastiadu" he wandered around fishing wadiyas and toddy shops with his ears wide open. Debriefing him at the wardroom bar revealed little about Marusinghe – except that he had never been sighted on the coast.

Police Intelligence from Colombo now entered the act as Marusinghe's name had kept cropping up in interrogations. A pleasant young man visited me, looking mild and un-police-like, sent by HQ to look for Marusinghe. His cover story for walking around the jungle was that he was a Forest Officer. One night, in utmost secrecy he brought me his star informant, a bearded Moulana from the Muslim village of Rotaweva on the road to Anuradhapura. He swore that a youth, who fitted Marusinghe's description, was occasionally seen on jungle foot paths on the way to chena cultivation. He believed that this youth had even bought provisions from a wayside kiosk. Aa good lead, we thought. The Navy mounted a textbook counter-guerrilla operation. The bearded informant (code named Castro) to his great joy, was togged up in Navy blues and helmet to conceal his identity. He led them here, he led them there, he led them everywhere, but the quarry was nowhere. A dispirited patrol returned at dusk and a devalued informant reluctantly surrendered his uniform.

Sources of information gradually dried up. The Services now took every rumour with more than a grain of salt. As months passed, the insurgency petered out, the roads opened and Trinco was no longer a town under siege. It became increasingly difficult to believe in a man who had never really been seen and an insurgent who had never mounted any attack.

Finale ?

Many months later I led a team of Kachcheri officials on the biennial trek (by jeep, of course) through the thick jungle of Seruwila to the tobacco lands of Kompanachchi on the banks of the Mahaweli bordering the grasslands of Polonnaruwa. Our hosts were tall and taciturn Muslims, breeders of graceful white long-horned cattle. Sharing their simple, but ample, lunch we got talking. Our Land Overseer had heard a vague story of Marusinghe having been sighted in this area, headed towards Polonnaruwa. We questioned our hosts about this possibility. They replied that no unarmed man, unfamiliar with this elephant and bear infested jungle could ever make such a journey. However, they added, some months earlier they had come across a skeleton crushed by an elephant. It would not have been a local man as no villager had ever gone missing.

The hunt for Marusinghe had ended. Never had so many, hunted for so long for – nothing ?

Tailpiece

Over twenty-five years had passed. In Colombo I was meeting a team from one of the major international agencies based in Washington. Among them was an expat Sri Lankan agronomist, plump, greying, with a naggingly familiar face. He seemed briefly startled to see me, but settled down as the discussion got under way. As the team left he looked quizzically at me and said "Weren't you the G.A. Trincomalee in 1971 ? I don't think we ever met – my name is ..... Marusinghe !"

"FARAWAY PLACES WITH STRANGE SOUNDING NAMES"

Unusual names of villages and towns in our homeland have "held me in thrall" ever since my school Principal in Ratnapura's Sivali Vidyalaya sixty years ago, inspired me to write an essay to the school magazine on "Place Names associated with Animals". I remember revelling in place names such as Kabara-gala, Mee-mure, Walas-mulla and the like. This interest lay dormant while I ambled through a degree in English and French at the University where I *"sauntered, played or rioted, talked unprofitably into the small hours and read lazily in trivial books" (Wordsworth).*

Trees and the Sinhalese

My interest in place names perked up again ten years later when I started working as a District Land Officer in many Kachcheries all over the island, hiking along tank bunds, jungle trails and mountain paths on field visits to distant villages. I will always remember Gomarankadawala, 'tank where the sambhur was killed', in Trincomalee District, as the place that rekindled my abiding interest in place names. And it was during these wanderings that I developed my conviction that the pre-Buddhist Sinhala people were tree worshippers. I observed that the vast majority of the names of Sinhala villages derive from the names of trees.

Bambalapitiya retains the memory of the 'jambola' trees that once flourished here. Dehi-wela, Bo-pe, Madam-pe, Pihimbiya-gollewa, Moragaha-mulla, and many, many other towns and villages are named after trees that once grew there. Something in the Sinhala psyche made the original settlers name their homes after their arboreal neighbours (and gods?). I have also observed that almost every title deed describes boundaries after trees e.g. N – Kesel-watta, E – Ambagaha-wela, S – Siyambala-watta, W – Kos-watta.

Two more facts seem to support my (unproven and unscholarly) theory. The first is the theme of Arahat Mahinda's first sermon to King Tissa – on the mango tree. The second is the great veneration Sinhala Buddhists pay to the Bo tree, which is grown in every Vihara in Sri Lanka – but hardly ever seen in temples in Thailand. It is tragic that today's uninspiring clusters of G.I roofed cottages are arrogantly named after ephemeral politicos (e.g. X-gama, Y-pura or Z-nagar) who allocated government funds to build them. The trees are now no more, felled for timber by these very politicoes and/or their henchmen. I now rest my amateur theorising and leave the field to scholars of the Sinhala language, our history and botany.

Boers and Boulders

On circuit in the Bentara Walallawita Korale of Galle District, I was fascinated to find the village of Kurundu-gaha-hetekma named after the milepost located by an unusually large cinnamon tree. Kilometers have now replaced miles and I wonder whether the tree and the old milepost, after which the village was named, yet remain. But the charming name, at least, will last for it was announced that the new expressway will pass alongside.

Not too far from there is Uragas-manhandiya – 'junction of ura trees'. At that time I wasn't that curious to inquire as to what exactly these oddly named trees were, or look for them. They remain relegated to that vast store of knowledge I will never have access to – to join such mysteries as black holes and Mayan hieroglyphics. What really fascinated me here was my 'discovery' of a little known camp for Boer prisoners of war in the late 1890s. I remember inspecting the crumbling barracks they had once occupied. And I remembered an old Sinhala jingle which 'enshrined' (wrong word) a memory of these lusty Boers.

Uragasmanhandiya
(From "Kavata Kathikaya" 1895)

My free translation follows:

"Tara rara Boom-de-yay
From Uragas man handiyay
Randy Boers are on the way,
Lock up your sisters,
Don't let them stray!"

I do not think all doors were barred that firmly, for I did meet on my inspections a few old countrymen with corn-coloured hair and bright blue eyes in their nut brown faces.

Somewhere near Pitigala, or so I seem to recall, a huge boulder jutted on to a narrow rural road compelling drivers to make a blind turn round it. Driving along with the Village Headman (an extinct species) who was a fountain of local lore, I learnt the strange name bestowed on that bend in the road, and the reason for it. This was "Chevlet Vanguva" named after an extraordinary event in the 1930s when two enormous Chevrolet automobiles crashed head-on while negotiating the bend from opposite sides. Villagers from far and near flocked to see this fantastic sight – and the elephants who tugged the cars apart. As cars were made of sterner stuff in those pioneer days, there were no casualties in either car, one belonging to a Mudaliyar and the other to a white planter. As I chronicle this scrap of local history I wonder whether the boulder and the bend, with that most unforgettable name, yet remain. If not, let this note serve as their epitaph.

A Jester, an Ogre and a Noblewoman

Among the pastimes I indulged during my drives, along the 160 miles that distanced Trincomalee from Colombo, was to read signboards to detect quaint English and piquant misspellings. Passing through Matale District, one of the few where I was never stationed, I came across a signpost pointing towards "Kavataya-bendi-amuna"

– Anicut built by the Jester. What a wonderful name, I thought, imagining a Jester (a la Andare) of the Royal Court who used his wealth to build this anicut to irrigate the fields of his natal village. I never learnt his name, but his title and generosity remain enshrined for ever in the name bestowed on the little dam he built for his people.

A few days ago I read of the restoration of an ancient irrigation canal with the intriguing name of "Yaka-bendi-ela" – canal built by the Ogre. I am afraid I do not know where this is located. And I wonder whether there is a folk tale of an ogre who built this either because he was kind-hearted, or was compelled to do so by the trickery of a wily peasant, who abound in village yarns. Or, on the other hand, does it carry a faint folk memory of its builders, the pre-Vijayan people of Lanka whom later arrivals dubbed 'Yakas'?

In the jungles of Anuradhapura, along the old road that led from Trincomalee there was the village of "Parangiya-wadiya" – camp of the (White) Foreigner. I never got to find the origin of this name. One theory, popular in the Kachcheri, is that King Rajasinghe's soldiers camped there en route to Kandy, while escorting Robert Knox and his fellow English sailors, who had been shipwrecked on Kandyan territory in Mutur. Interestingly this well-documented fact belies the present claim of a "traditional homeland" in Trincomalee, concocted by Tamils of recent domicile.

Not very far from here, off the road from Horowpotana, huddled the humble homes of the little village rejoicing in the strangely romantic name of "Tikiri-Handewa" – Evening of the Noblewoman. I was fortunate enough, some forty years ago, to meet some old peasants who told me how the village earned its name. In a time long ago, a young noblewoman was being escorted in a palanquin, towards her walauwa in Anuradhapura. They party had met some mishap on the way – possibly a palanquin pole that had snapped (like poor Dona Catherina's, some centuries earlier) – which delayed their journey. As dusk fell the party arrived at a little cluster of huts huddled together in the dark and looming jungle.

The exhausted group spoke to the timid villagers, who had never before met any official of importance, and asked them for a night's shelter for their noble lady and her escort. One can imagine the trembling and excitement with which the villagers rallied round to clean up their largest hut for their noble guest, which the escort hung with white awnings to keep creepy crawlies off her bedding. They would have offered her their meagre food, such as dried venison and wild honey, which she is sure to have relished as a change from the blander cuisine of the walauwa. And she must have spoken to them with gratitude and sweet condescension. Next morning she left for home with her escort – but left behind the memory of her gracious stay which the village honoured by naming their hitherto nameless settlement after this unforgettable event. The fragrance of that memory wafts across the centuries whenever one hears that name.

Trees and Waterways

A truly historic, centuries old, tree is now no more – felled by a cyclone some years ago. This was the legendary "Oru-bendi-siyambalawa" – the Tamarind on which boats were moored. This massive tree stood on the banks of the Amban Ganga in Polonnaruwa and its rugged trunk was scarred by the ropes of canoes that had moored alongside for centuries. As a schoolboy, I remember being photographed by my father, as I fingered the ancient scars and tried to imagine the boatmen of Parakramabahu ferrying goods to the royal capital of Polonnaruwa. Alas, history in schools has now been felled like that grand old tree.

Far South, on the banks of the Walawe soared a massive gnarled 'kumbuk' tree, a tree of iron-hard, saw-breaking timber that grows by rivers and reservoirs. To me it is memorable for one thing – that is the cruelly apt name it earned on account of its singular appearance "Barawa-kumbuka" 'the Kumbuk with elephantiasis'. Its trunk did resemble the grossly swollen leg with huge overlapping flaps of a giant suffering from filariasis.

As an undergraduate in the late 1940s I spent a holiday in Bintenna where R.B.Ratnayake reigned as Divisional Revenue Officer over a huge area where many genuine Veddhas yet lived, and were often found dressed in 'amudays' and clutching deer-skin pouches, squatting on his verandah seeking redress. He had also inherited an "official horse" – a hangover from colonial days when field officers rode these hardy steeds up the rocky hills and down the stony dales on their inspections. R.B. never rode his horse and it grew fat lazily munching on the wild grass of his paddock.

One day we set out on a long hike to Mahiyangana, the outermost boundary of his kingdom. We spent the night in the open verandah of a Rural Court house. I was entranced by the pitch dark, only enlivened by fireflies' twinkling glimmer, the occasional hoot of a hunting owl and the distant plaintive chant of 'pel kavi' by chena farmers. It was on this hike, which was a foretaste of my own working life yet to come, that I came across the most sweetly onomatopoeic name of any stream crossing – 'Gadugudawa'. Old Tennyson himself would have been happy to hear this Sinhala vocalisation of the turbulent gurgling of a rock strewn stream.

Bones and Fines

The little market-town of Nochchiyagama, is a few miles from Anuradhapura on the road west to Puttalam. Its name is notable for the fact that it honours the pioneer settler 'Nochchi' or 'Nochchiya' who founded the village long, long ago. This is a name once popular among some of the so-called 'lower' castes in the traditional hierarchy. What is significant is that this name has been retained with no attempt to "sex it up" (to use a topical phrase) by judicious alteration. This is, I like to believe, characteristic of old Sinhala culture, epitomised by the fact that our first, and greatest, capital was named after Anuradha, the chieftain who founded it. Our greatest kings ruled from this city but never exhibited the 'hubris' to name it after their royal selves. Nochchiyagama is, thus, very much in the great tradition.

Not far from Nochchiyagama is the quaintly named village of "Kukul-katuwa" – 'chicken bone'! I have, unfortunately, not the slightest idea of the tale behind this intriguing name. There is another, and better known 'katuwa' in Puttalam District, and even figured in some land scam where VIPs were involved. This is "Arachchi-katuwa" Headman's Bones! I wonder whether it has been named after a Village Headman of yore whose unquiet bones lie there!.

Some miles North of Padeniya, in Kurunegala District, I halted my car in a quiet forest to buy some of the assorted vegetables that village folk displayed on rickety tables to tempt passers-by driving through. I idly inquired as to the name of the village. "Kasi-kotay" I was told – 'stub of a coin'. I had never, ever heard such a name and insisted on hearing the tale behind the name. Long ago, in the early British Colonial era this village was run by a strong-willed Headman. However, the authorities once accused him of some petty transgression and hauled him before the English Magistrate. The Headman conducted his own defence and won his acquittal. But the Magistrate, to save the Prosecuting Officer's face, imposed a nominal fine of an absurdly low value – half a 'kasi'. The smallest coin in the Headman's pouch was one 'kasi'. He took it out, then pulled out his 'giray' (nut-cracker) from his betel pouch and crunched the 'kasi' into two! One half he placed on the astounded Court Mudaliyar's tatble. He pocketed the other half and triumphantly returned to his village. His fellow villagers were so proud of his derring-do that they promptly re-named itself 'Kasi-kotay' to record this deed, perhaps "till sun and moon endure" as the old kings inscribed in stone.

A Plea

These are but the random memories of an inquisitive field officer in his 'anecdotage'. But I hope I have whetted the scholarly curiosity of students and scholars from fields such as history, linguistics, botany and even geology, to undertake a multi-disciplinary study of old Sinhala place names before they are swamped by those of politicians.

GOODBYE G.A !

News Item: "On 1st January, 1993 the twenty-five Government Agents of Districts were replaced by 250 Divisional Secretaries."

The New Year dawned in '93, midst explosive din,
Alas! within the Residencies the mood was dark and grim.
Those mansions vast, on spacious lawns, on hill-tops,
sun-kissed shore
Lay bereft and forlorn, as G.A.s rose no more.

For close upon one hundred years they ruled the countryside
Agents of a Raj, now gone, puffed with viceregal pride
Resplendent in their ostrich plumes, they governed humble
blacks
From Kachcheries, with Mudaliyars, and clerks with files
in stacks.
No wonder they were loath to go
When Britannia ruled no more.

The new lords of The Residencies, true sons of Lanka's soil
Booted out cook-appus, 'bistake' and Yorkshire pud.
The aroma of bacon, gave way to coconut oil
As 'kussiammas' toiled and moiled to dish up native food.

Assistants for his office work, for lands, co-ops and food,
For poor relief, for festivals, they helped as best they could
The G.A. at his many tasks. They were a motley army,
Some were bad and some were good, but quite a few
were barmy!

Seated at their polished desks, they signed away at permits
For guns, for paddy, lands and water; liquor shops and logs.
But, latterly, their time was spent in honouring Members' chits
The sad and bitter truth was that – they had become only cogs
- Though cogs with cars and flags and perks
Their role was that of humble clerks.

Their sun had set, their day was done. In their faltering footsteps
With vim, vigour and confidence strode the people's reps
Who MUCH preferred a smaller cog to be at call and beck
So every Division has today, a Divisional Sec.

Good bye! Government Agent. Farewell! an age that was.
The up and coming D.S. has sent them all to grass.

Like the dew on the mountain, the foam on the river,
Like the peel of a banana, they have gone – and for ever.

BACK TO HORSESHOE STREET

Over sixty years later Kandy's Cross Street has changed surprisingly little. Traffic crowds the once-quiet road which was our childhood playground. The 'aeroplane trees' have long since been felled, and a massive Secretariat has replaced the rambling colonial bungalows that sheltered beyond the boundary wall of 'our' road. Miraculously, however, the home of our distant, magic childhood yet stands firm, with its antiquity now honoured with a plaque by the Central Cultural Fund.

Our home yet stands, now honoured as a World Heritage site

Also by Tissa Devendra

Travel	Sri Lanka: The Emerald Island
Short Stories	Tales from the Provinces
For Children	Princes, Peasants and Clever Beasts More Princes, Peasants and Clever Beasts